To Mrs
Bena'

Thank you for all
your support !!

Knowledge Is Power

What Everyone Should Know About The Police

Dr. Dani Lee Harris

Dr. Dani Lee
Harris

ISBN-13: 978-1508475538

ISBN-10: 1508475539

www.drdanileeharris.org

DEDICATION

I dedicate this book to every officer that lost their life in the line of duty. The job of an officer is thankless and at times unappreciated. I consider these brave men and women of the thin blue line family, guardian angels of those left behind to protect and serve this country. The ultimate sacrifice of giving your life while serving should never be forgotten. I salute you, I thank you, and I honor your legacy. To the families of fallen officers, I thank you for sharing and then losing a loved one in the name of service. May your pain be comforted, if just a little, by knowing your family member showed the ultimate meaning of love.

I also dedicate this book to every member of our society that has lost their life by the hands of an officer. Nothing I can say will bring comfort to the families for what some may see as an unjustifiable loss, a senseless death. I wish I could bring some solitude to your pain, understanding to your heart and comfort to your soul. I can't bring your loved ones back; I just wish to make it better with the words I spill on the following pages. I wish to bring understanding and peace between the community and the police in order to save lives. To save the life of another person, whether officer or civilian.

To every person that puts on a uniform to represent a law enforcement agency across this country, I dedicate this book to you and your families. I understand the training, the sweat, the tears, the victories and the losses you have had to endure to be among America's Finest and I salute you, I thank you and I honor you.

Contents

ACKNOWLEDGMENTS

I want to take a moment and acknowledge the people that helped me get through this book and this process. I wrote this book in six weeks and it would not have been possible without the assistance of my wife Latasha Davis-Harris. I thank you for your constant support and sacrifice. You are my ride/die and I love you with every fiber in me. I want to thank our sons for their support. Jason, Dante and Erion, I love you with all that I have in me. To my siblings, Tanisha, Tia, Martha, and Christopher, I thank you. To my siblings on my Father's side, since it is too many to name, I will thank all of you. I love each of you. To my Mother-in-law and my Father-in-law, Glenda and Eric James, you guys are the best, thank you for your support. To my Marketing Manager J.L. King, without you pushing me, I have no idea how long it would have taken me to finish. I thank you. To my best friends Nic and Kimberly, you guys rock and I thank you for all your support and encouragement. "Sleep is for suckers". I love you to life.

Introduction

I purposely do not mention the Police Department I work for in order to make it clear that the words of this book come from me and not my department. I am not representing any organization with the publishing of this book. I use my personal experiences, the experiences of other officers from different departments and research conducted by myself. All research conducted for this book used scholarly sources to ensure accuracy and maintain written integrity.

In light of some unfortunate events in the media spotlight, I have decided to write this book. This book is not necessarily about right or wrong relating to police work, but its intent is to outline some matters that will equip people with knowledge of police culture, clear up some misunderstandings, and give a perspective from a Black, Police Officer with an 18 year history in the field, otherwise; a seldom heard from viewpoint. I was raised to believe that if you are not part of the solution, then you are part of the problem. It is so easy to stand on the sidelines and scream about injustices, unfair acts and racism among the file and ranks of policing. Just like any other profession or career, there is the good, the bad, and the ugly. In writing this book, I wish to provide some information that will educate some, further the knowledge or others and simultaneously provide knowledge to those with little or no knowledge of the police way.

For the last 12 years, I have called Metro Atlanta home. Living 22 miles outside the city limits, I moved here by way of New York City. I was born in the Bronx and raised in Spanish Harlem until the age of 12, at which time my siblings, and I moved throughout every borough in New York due to placement within the foster-care system. Mostly living in poverty stricken neighborhoods, I grew up with a deep resentment for officers of the law. Seeing the "man" in the neighborhood usually was not a pleasant experience. More often than not, the officers did not mirror the ethnic community in which I resided. Overseeing interactions between members of my community and the police left me feeling as if they just did not understand the way things worked in our hood. The occasions, in which they were called to deal directly with my family, I always felt as if we were bothering them, and they did not care to assist us. Hearing communication between my Mother and the police made me feel as if they thought she was ignorant, stupid or both. My Mother, the Late Carole Ann Nelson was an unpublished author that was a well-read intellectual. Demeaning is the word I use, to sum up the feeling that I was left with after interactions with the police. Kind, gentle, understanding, respectful and patient are not words that I would have ever associated with law enforcement at that time.

I was told by my maternal grandfather that we had a lot of people in my family that wore the law enforcement hat, and he always said it with such pride. Every time I heard these statements, I would cringe at the thought of my family being a part of such a hostile group of people. It wasn't until I worked as an Evening Teen Coordinator in my late teens when I developed relationships with officers who would start to shape a different perspective of cops for me. One of New York's finest, a white officer in his late twenties and I became particularly familiar with one another as he patrolled the area in which I worked. One particular conversation the officer looked at me and said "you would make a great officer." I almost spit out the liquids I had just placed in my mouth. My reaction stunned him as I replied "I would never be a pig." This statement led to many conversations and debates about policing, the culture and my deep resentment for officers. This officer would come by my workplace every day and hold long conversations with me, often clearing up a lot of misconceptions I came to adopt from the streets. In my mid-twenties, I joined the law enforcement family and now, eighteen years later. I am on the other side of this pen attempting to clear up some misconceptions and further knowledge of the readers of this book.

Chapter 1: Dear officer

"The art and science of asking questions is the source of all knowledge" Thomas Berger

This chapter is a collection of letters sent to me, about different situations and scenarios that the sender encountered while dealing with Law Enforcement. I answer the letters, bringing clarity about how officers think, and are trained. This platform also serves to inform civilians of their personal rights within each scenario. Please understand that each situation is unique, and although you may have a similar situation, the outcome may not yield the same results. Each state has their laws, and each department has their own Standard Operating Procedure that governs what actions are taken in situations. It is important that you as a civilian are acquainted with your local police department by getting involved in community settings such as town-hall meetings. Each state also has their laws published so you can find them on the web. In the technological age we live in, anyone with access to a smart phone, computer, and the internet can look up state and city laws.

I have given the letter writers pseudonyms to protect their identity. The structure of the letters has been changed to correct grammatical errors and sentence structure. The demographics are indeed factual, so the laws discussed are applicable to that particular situation and area. I must remind you that each scenario has many factors that contribute to the outcome. For one, each scenario has a different person who thinks, speaks, and acts according to their personality, and their individuality. This is the reason why nothing is routine in the work of a police officer on the streets. Different people, with a different mindset = different results

Question (1) Domestic: My name is Darryl, and I live in Atlanta. My girlfriend and I share an apartment together. One night recently, we were having an argument, and it became physical. My girlfriend threw a glass bowl at me (which broke and cut me). I shoved her down on the couch, and she pulled a knife out the draw. I started laughing at her and grabbed her, as I was pulling back from her, I cut my arm with the knife. One of the neighbors called the police and when they arrived (one black female cop and one white male cop), my girlfriend was taken to jail. I told the officers what took place and so did my girlfriend. I also told the officer that I was not pressing charges, and they stated they did not care. How can the officers arrest her without my permission?

Answer (1): In most states, domestic violence is not tolerated and has laws to prove such. There was a time in our society when officers would arrive on disputes and if no one was pressing charges, the officers would kindly go about their business. With the amount of people being killed in domestic incidences across the nation most states have adopted laws to protect civilians from domestic abuse. With this being said, officers respond to domestic calls and interviews all parties involved. In this particular situation, there were cuts to prove an altercation. Once an officer can determine that a physical altercation has occurred, the next step is to determine who the primary aggressor is. This evaluation is done by talking to each person individually and observing the evidence on the scene (If there is any). From the story you shared, your girlfriend was the primary aggressor and caused harm to your person. Escalating a situation, such as pulling something out that can be used as a weapon (such as a knife) does show aggression. In most states, officers take the following into consideration when on a domestic call, statements from parties, extent of personal injuries, evidence that someone acted in self-defense, prior complaints of domestic abuse to name a few. The State would be the complainant, so they don't need anyone else to press charges anymore.

Question (2) Traffic: I am Andre, and I reside in Forest Park Georgia. I was pulled over by a Police officer, and he said it was for a broken tail light. My tail light was broken; however, I was asked to get out of the car and put my hands up on the top of the roof. I was riding alone and had not done anything wrong except have a broken light. The officer asked me where I was coming from and where I was going, while squeezing my pockets. I asked the officer if what he was doing was necessary, and he said, "yes, for my safety and yours." I had a bag of food on my passenger seat, and the officer asked me what was in my bag. I told him food. He then got the bag from the seat and looked into it. I was allowed back in my car and received a ticket and let go. I was left to wonder if what happened to me and the way it happened was legal.

Answer (2) Traffic: I first want to point out that I appreciate this letter not identifying the race of the officer. In a case where the initial contact is legal, it really doesn't matter the race of the officer. You acknowledge that the officer had the right to pull you over because you did have a broken light on your vehicle. If indeed you were informed to exit the vehicle, this is not an uncommon practice for some officers. If an officer feels more comfortable with you outside the vehicle, they may ask you to step out. Once you are out of the vehicle, a quick check to make sure you are not armed and dangerous is legal only if the officer can articulate why they felt you may be armed or dangerous. A frisk is allowed by law when an officer believes you may be armed, dangerous, or involved in criminal activity (even if the officer is suspicious of your passengers). Now in order for an officer to search your vehicle WITHOUT your permission, they would have to have a reasonable basis to believe you or your passengers are involved in criminal activity, better known as probable cause. You can give an officer a reason to suspect something by reaching under your seat, moving around a lot in the vehicle before the officer approaches you, etc. Another way an officer can

13

search your vehicle WITHOUT your permission or consent is if they observe something in plain sight in your vehicle that is illegal. Example of this is a weapon on a seat, illegal or suspected illegal drugs in plain sight, etc. Remember, if an officer does not have a reason to believe you may be armed and dangerous; they can simply ask to check your person and/or your vehicle. If you give them permission, then anything stemming from that search is legal. If you or any passenger is arrested, an "inventory" search of the vehicle can be conducted without any suspicion.

If you are stopped by an officer, and they ask you if they can search your vehicle, you do have the legal right to verbally state to the officer "I do not consent to a search of my car or person." Again, this would only work in your favor if there is no probable cause for the officer to search your vehicle. Say, for example, you are stopped and an officer smells what he suspects to be an illegal substance (fresh), the officer can search your vehicle. If a police drug dog walking by your car and the dog "hit" that something is wrong (that would be probable cause), this allows the officer to legally search your vehicle. In the case of this question, without any further information, the officer did not have the legal right to retrieve the bag to search it. I was not on the scene, and some information may be missing, but as it stands by the story shared, I have to say no, it was not a legal search.

Question (3) Street Stop: I am Rodney and I am a black male, age 24. I was walking down the street in a black neighborhood (NYC) at around 10pm in the summer. A black officer approached me and started asking me questions. I was asked where was I coming from, where was I going, where do I live? I admit I was a little agitated for being stopped and questioned just for walking down the street, so I did get smart with the officer. I asked him why was he stopping me, what had I done wrong and why he was asking me personal questions? When I did not want to answer the officers' questions, he demanded that I produce identification, or else I would be going to jail. I gave the officer my ID, and he ran it through his system and eventually let me go. Was this stop legal?

***Answer* (3) Street Stop:** Yes, an officer can stop and question you. The law gives officers certain rights in order for them to perform their duty of protecting the community, civilians, and property. There are three levels in which an officer can engage you. The first level is consensual, when both parties are just having a conversation willingly (you do not have to engage in conversation if you do not desire to). The next level is investigative detention; when an officer has a reasonable, articulate suspicion that the person stopped was involved in illegal activity. Investigative detention does not involve choice by the person detained. The last level is when an officer is actually arresting someone. This is when the person does not have the liberty to leave the situation, and the officer has probable cause to apprehend the person. Probable cause is more than reasonable articulate suspicion. Probable cause is more than suspicions, but is established through factual evidence. If you are suspected of something, officers have a duty to inform you of such. NO you do not have to NECESSARY answer the police for you have the right to remain silent, and you have NO legal duty to answer any questions, which gives you the right to refuse to answer. However, under normal circumstances it is probably favorable for civilians to cooperate with law enforcement officers. There are times when a crime has been committed in the area, you may just fit the general description of person officers are looking for. Then there are times you may not fit any particular description, but an officer may think you may be able to assist in their investigation. The officer may or may not inform you that an investigation is underway.

As it relates to an officer asking for your identification, there are some states (24) that have stop-and-identify laws. Some states have laws that allow police to arrest a person who refuse to show identification. The catch to the Supreme Court case Hiibel v. Sixth Judicial District Court of Nevada is that in order for a civilian to HAVE to give up identification, the officer has to have a reasonable suspicion of criminal activity. The 24 states that have some form of stop-and-identify law are; Alabama, Arizona, Arkansas, Colorado, Delaware, Florida, Georgia, Illinois, Indiana, Kansas, Louisiana, Missouri (Kansas City only), Montana, Nebraska, Nevada, New Hampshire, New Mexico, New York, North Dakota, Ohio, Rhode Island, Utah, Vermont, and Wisconsin. Since each state law varies, it is a good idea to get familiar with the wording and meaning of the stop-and-identify law in your state.

Question (4) Driving under the influence, DUI: My name is Courtney, and I was arrested for DUI while sitting in my car outside my house (Jersey City). I was not driving the car; I was just sitting in the car listening to music. A police car pulled up beside me, and the officer said she had received a noise complaint and asked me what I was doing. I told her I was just listening to my music. The officer asked me if I had been drinking, and I told her yes inside my house and pointed to the house. I told the officer that my roommate was in the house sleeping, and I wanted to listen to my music, so I came outside to sit in my car. I was told to get out of my car and given a sobriety test, which I suppose I failed. I was then taken to jail. I am still going back and forth on this case, and I really don't understand how I could go to jail for DUI when I was not driving.

Answer (4) DUI: The fact that the officer received a complaint in that area and investigating a situation, it was in her right to stop and question you. You may have been playing the music loud enough to draw attention to your area. When the officer asked you about drinking, and you confirmed her suspicion, it was also in her right to administer a field sobriety test. The law in many states makes it clear that you can be detained, questioned, identified and arrested if you are "IN CONTROL" of a motor vehicle. Many states have laws that describe when a person has actual physical control of a vehicle, even if the vehicle is not being moved at the time, the same rules of the road applies. The meaning of actual physical control are as follows for most state laws (please check your state law for specifics), if the vehicle is on/off, is the vehicle operable, where the keys in or out of the ignition, was there any gas in the tank, was the defendant behind the driver's seat, just to name a few. Most people would reasonably think that simply being behind the wheel is not enough to constitute physical control of the vehicle, if the vehicle is not on and the gears of the vehicle activated. This is why it is important to be informed on matters in which you can easily be affected. I would suggest you obtain an attorney that specializes in DUI cases and have them explain details with you as it relates to the specifics of your case.

Question (5) Same-Sex Domestic Violence: Hello officer, my name is Mat, and I am a gay white male. Recently, my partner and I were having a heated argument in our home, and my partner called the police. When the police arrived, everything had calmed down, and we were separated and questioned in two different rooms of our home. This was a small fight, and my partner did have a scratch on his arm, and I had one on my face. After being questioned, we both were arrested, I tried to talk to both officers and ask them why we both were going to jail and one of them stated, "since you are both males, we cannot determine who the primary aggressor is, so we will let the judge figure it out." I clearly informed the officers that I was the one who started the argument and fight and my partner stated the same. They still took us both to jail. This caused my partner to lose his very good-paying job. Now we are left to pay legal fees when my partner was the only person in our home working. I am livid with the fact that officers are not better trained to deal with same-sex domestic calls. Why did we both have to go to jail?

Answer (5) Same-Sex Domestic Violence: If indeed the situation happened as expressed, this sounds like a difficult situation. The truth of it is that officers across the country are getting better training with dealing with same-sex domestic calls. Part of the determination as to whether or not someone is the primary aggressor on a domestic call, is to identify the person that has "more" power or can control the situation more than the other. Unfortunately in the case of same sex, this determination most often cannot be made, especially if both people are comparable in size, and weight. I have been trained to determine the primary aggressor and this does not depend upon the sex, size or weight of a person. After interviewing both parties, usually a determination of who the primary aggressor is can be made. Since you did not mention what state, this happened in, I cannot tell you what the local laws say specifically for your state. The fact that both of you sustained some type of injury, would justify the officers taking both of you to jail since no one explained the injuries (if that is the case) I do know that most all law enforcement personnel across the country are trained to identify the primary aggressor in a domestic call. Domestic can include siblings who share the same residence, parents who share a child (do not have to live together), a spouse, former spouse or former household member and those in a dating relationship.

Since you stated that you and your partner both stated that you were the primary aggressor in your situation, you really did take the decision out of the hands of the officer and frankly, you should have been charged as the primary aggressor, and this is just my opinion based on what you have expressed in your letter. Since this did not happen, once the case is determined by a judge or jury, the case against your partner will be determined according to the evidence and facts presented in the case against him. It seems as if you have already obtained legal advice, and that is what I would have advised in this situation. More importantly, violence of any kind is never ok. In my opinion "love does not hit "something to think about.

Question (6) Questioned by Police: I am a 20-year-old black man. I go by the name Bones on the street. I was home chilling with my girl, and the police came banging on my door. When my girl answered the door, the police asked for me. I was told by one of the officers that I needed to come by the police station to answer some questions about a recent murder. I did go to the police station to talk to them. I was held for 18 hours and harassed by the officers as if I was the murderer. The officers lied to me and told me that they had a couple of witnesses who placed me at the scene of the murder. I was nowhere near the murder, and the person murdered was a good friend of mine. I have been threatened and had to move, because of all the lies being told on the streets. I was cleared on the murder rap, but my life will never be the same. How can it be ok for officers to lie on you and mess up your life just because they don't know who to go after?

Answer (6) Questioned by Police: I think the question is "do police officers lie" and if yes why and how are they allowed to do this. Well, the truth of the matter is that police are allowed to use deception during an investigation as long as the deception does not coerce a person into confessing to a crime they didn't commit. Remember you do not have to answer any questions without the presence of an attorney. Say you agree to speak to the police, and then you feel as if the police are being deceptive with you and you begin to feel uneasy. At that point or at any point throughout the investigation, you want to end the line of questioning, you can stop answering and request an attorney. What you will be doing is invoking your Fifth Amendment right to remain silent and at this time you can request an attorney. Then remain silent until your request has been granted, and you are allowed to speak to your attorney.

Deception includes statements like "if you don't confess to this crime, I am going to do this." I know of a case where a young lady was threatened with her children. The officer told her that if she did not confess to being a part of a robbery, her children were going to be taken from her and never returned. This young lady did confess to the crime; it was determined that the officer used deceptive coercion, and the case against her was dropped. However, the case took a lot from this woman and even years later, she is still struggling to get her life on track. If an attorney was present, I do believe there would have been a different result.

Again, these questions were answered using the facts presented in the letter. Dependent upon different facts and circumstances the results may be different. It is crucial that civilians understand their local laws and of course the state and federal laws that govern their situation.

Chapter 2: Real Talk 1 on 1

"I think I have come to a place where I'm able to feel more comfortable about being honest" June Jordan

This chapter is specifically dedicated to the black community of America. I am excited to be able to talk to you and express my views, hopes and dreams for our community. There will be some that will not understand where I am coming from, and frankly, you may go away from reading this chapter wishing to "agree to disagree" and this is perfectly ok. I would like for you to employ an open mind, a clear heart and free spirit in order to catch the message and not just be quick to shoot the messenger. This entire book is dedicated to empowerment, and I wish to do the same here within the pages for this chapter. So after reading this chapter let it become a topic of conversation at your next book club or social gathering. This is truly the intent of this chapter.

I chose to use the term "black community" instead of "African American," for I have learned that not everyone in the community identifies with "African" and for that reason alone I chose not to use that term. This chapter will bring in a little history, explore some myths, examine some truths and allow a platform for effective communication to take root. It is important to know that I am speaking from my experiences, conversations with other members of the black community, research that has been conducted to understand topics, and personal interviews with friends and family members. My intent with the words from these pages, is to plant a seed, and hopefully birth community reflection, honest evaluations and self-accountability. So grab you a cup of your favorite beverage, and snack and please get ready to hear me. Then hopefully meaningful, thought provoking and life-changing conversations can occur within our communities.

I Cry, You Cry

As I decided to write this book, there is presently a lot going on in the media as it relates to tension between the police departments and the black communities across the country. It is hard being an officer of color right now, and this is just the truth. I always feel the need to be on the defense, or making sure to have prepared answers and statements for the comments and questions that I would be flurried with from black community members. I Sense the need to take a stance on either side, the pressure of having to choose a side. Well, I decided not to choose any side, instead of standing to one side or the other and slinging rocks; I choose to stay in the middle and bring peace, understanding and knowledge. With that being said, I want to state that I cry, just as a lot of the black community sheds tears with the loss of lives. Regardless of color, it is hard to see the loss of life no matter the circumstance. I do relate to the anger, I do relate to the pain, and I do understand the outrage. What I do not understand is the selectiveness of when these emotions are employed. What do I mean by that.....Well I mean we don't get hurt enough, we don't get angry enough, maybe we are not pained enough. I know this sounds a little off right now, but the words I speak have to be stated.

People, why are we not angered about the fact that MOST black males are killed by members of their community. This is not unique to just the black race, for most people in the United States are killed by someone they know. Black people are dying by the hands of their brothers and sisters period. Now we can always point the finger and start discussing why this is happening, who is to blame for it and the origins of the chaos, but seriously where is that going to get us? Will pointing the finger and getting indignant about why we are killing each other get us to stop the violence tomorrow, I think not. I can no longer stand back and watch people shy away from speaking the truth. Where and when did it become a problem to self-reflect? Is that not what we try to teach our children? Do we teach them to think about their actions, absolutely. We teach them to understand there are consequences behind their actions. We help them to be responsible, so why is it a problem to scream "STOP KILLING YOUR BROTHERS AND SISTERS AND GETTING UPSET WHEN PEOPLE TALK ABOUT IT." The most important thing to do is acknowledge the truth and find a way to correct the problem.

Now it is very important to understand that black people killing other black people is not unique to race. Studies show that most murders are committed by people who know each other, also known as interracial killings. The 2012 Federal Bureau of Investigations expanded report states the following (Hispanics are included as White in this report) There were a total of 14,581 murders. The race of the *murder offenders* are broken down as such; white: 4,582 (31.4%), black: 5,531 (37.9), other: 240 (1.6%), and unknown: 4,228 (29.0%). *Murder victims* were broken down as such; white: 5,855, black: 6,454, other: 326, and unknown: 130. The following numbers are race of victim and race of the offender. These numbers show the interracial murders I referred to previously. Race of victim white: 3,128, race of offender: (w) = 2,314/ (b) = 431/ (o) = 36/ (u) = 47. For black victims: 2,648, race of offender: (w) = 193/ (b) = 2,412/ (o) = 12/ (u) = 31. So if you read this correctly the number of known white people that killed black people = 193 and the number of known black people that killed white = 431. When it comes to cop killers in the FBI report, in 2012 51 offenders were identified with 48 law enforcement officers feloniously killed. The report stated 30 of the offenders were white, 16 were black, 1 was Indian/Alaska native, 1 Asian/pacific islander and the race of 3 offenders was unknown. I provide these statistics for your knowledge and encourage you to seek more information on subjects of this matter. In the end, it is the results that we see on paper that need to be addressed in the black communities. To seek a way to change the end results, we should be concerned with, looking for the WHY is this happening, and HOW DO WE STOP IT which is vital to addressing issues in the communities.

History of separation and resentment for each other

It is no secret that there is a division among the black communities. Again, we have to be honest and real in order to heal and grow. I remember growing up in Harlem, New York at a time when it was a problem to be black with light skin, or dark skin, too skinny, or overly thick. A time when the length and texture of your hair were always up for debate and discussion from the school yard among the youths to the project benches between the adults. There is no sanctity of being among one's own for the outsiders talked about you and so did your community. There is not one person of color that I have met or talked to that doesn't have a story about colourism, where light skin was better than dark skin. If you were lighter as a slave, you

31

were able to work indoors with more privileges, contrary to the dark-skin blacks who were confined to field work. This mentality fostered resentment among the black community and even today is still a topic of discussion. Now, this does not suggest the black communities alone is to blame for poor self-image. Media, over the years have also cultivated an atmosphere that promoted many myths about blacks. This division is much deeper today, where many black people feel like their own sisters and brothers try to keep them down. This is better known as the crabs in a barrel mentality. Where the lighter blacks look down on the darker, the rich look down on the poor, the educated vs. the uneducated, suburban communities shun the inner city communities and the list can go on and on, I think you get the point. There is no easy fix to this mentality but we can get better by first talking about the issue, then using our voices to speak up against poor image reflections in the media.

Where did good old-fashioned respect go?

In the black community, respect and loyalty has changed over the years. Let me say this, I do not think, nor believe that everything I say applies to everyone, but I am speaking of an overall perception. In certain cases, young people are not respecting their elders and the elders are not respecting the youths. Students do not seem to respect teachers as much as when I was growing up. Children do not fear discipline when it comes to respecting their parents. There was a time when it took a village to raise a child, now it seems as if everyone is forced to mind their own business and fear getting told off or worst. I am clear that this issue has a lot of *Buts*.....to go with why things have changed; I am simply pointing out the changes over time. In recent news, we see an outpour of anger about what police are doing in "our "communities. However, during these riots (and I am not implying all blacks) there were people of color that looted local businesses, burned their own properties and destroyed blocks upon blocks of businesses, and I say....the point of that is??? There is no justification for this type of behavior. The same businesses will take a lot of time and money to rebuild, if the owner decides to stay. The people that woke up without a job to go to, and unable to feed their families are affected by what some may call JUSTICE. I am sorry, but I do not and never will understand tearing down something in the name of justice. People, justice takes place in the voting poles, with your local city, state, House of Representatives and Congress leaders. Until we truly understand the power of election, we will never see change. Until we clearly see how powerful financial boycotting is we cannot gain a platform for reformation. Let us just remember how effective the Montgomery Boycott was at setting a platform for black voices to be heard. Financially crippling a mass-transit system will get people listening, I assure you.

Before we can unite to fight for justice, we have to respect and value one another lives. Remember black people are as strong as their weakest link. So instead of stepping or hating on one another, why not lend a helping hand. Help your neighborhood, your local schools, your county, and your city. Let us get the spirit of unity back, for our history shows that we had it at one time in this country. We don't have to spend too much time on the negative, but we can simply make a conscious decision to right the wrongs, accept our differences and remember the basis of what love is and what it looks like.

Judge not, lest ye be judged

There are many studies that point to the victim becoming the victimizer, and the abused becomes the abuser. For hundreds of years, the black community tried to liberate themselves from religious beliefs and even the words of the Bible that was used to oppress and keep the community segregated. However, today, the black communities are doing the same thing with others that do not resemble them. Yes, I am talking about the oppression of women and homosexuals in the black communities. For years, you were told that you were not equally intelligent, or you were less than equal as a human being. When there was discrimination towards blacks it was fought against, for oppression was not received well. So how can we then turn around and do the same thing that was done unto us.

This is not the platform I choose to speak about right, wrong, religion, or social expressions that lend its hand in the separation we see today. The point is to understand that separation and oppression are just that, no matter the receiving party. Christians, do not preach love and then turn around and judge your neighbor. No you do not have

35

to agree with someone's lifestyle or beliefs, but you are supposed to love them regardless. You are not supposed to judge others, and yes, you do this by talking or rather gossiping about folks business. Please stop living in glass houses and throwing stones. All have sinned and fallen short of the glory of God (for those that believe that). Show me a person that proclaims to know it all, have it all together and is perfect, and I will show you a liar! Agree to disagree and remember that you will not be the judge or jury of another person's life period. Stop the self-righteous rhetoric and remember LOVE. It is simple, yet we make it so complicated. If people do not agree with your religion, your views or your beliefs, it is ok. Our paths are so unique; that is why we were all made different. Respect other's differences and love them despite their race, their religion, sexual orientation, or any other difference. It is when we think WE are the only ones that is right and the ONLY ones with the answers for this thing called life; we run into conflict and turmoil. To prove a point, think and ask yourself this question "did I feel some type of way about what I read and now I feel some ill will" If your honest answer is yes, you are being judgmental and please don't

36

say anything about being righteous, for self-righteousness (having a certainty that one is totally correct or morally superior) is not favorable in the eyes of the Lord. "Some who trusted in themselves, that they were righteous, and treated others with contempt" Luke 18:9-14.

What some white people see but are afraid to say (this section was written from interviews taken with three anonymous white people, that wanted to be honest but were afraid of being identified. I have summed up their interviews and grouped together feelings, thoughts and observations that were similar to each other).

Do you believe in white privilege?

Anonymous white person #1 (28-year-old year old female): I was born and raised poor, so if you are asking in terms of economic status, I do not think of white privilege. However, if you are asking as far as me being a white person and having an advantage over a black person, then I would have to say yes. I am afforded opportunities that black people are not afforded simply because they were born black.

37

Anonymous white person #2 (47-year-old year old female): Yes, I believe in white privileged. I have always been in a position to observe how black people are denied things because of their race. Working in Human Resources for over 20 years, I have seen where a person wasn't given a chance of an interview because of their name or the area in which they live. So yes white privilege does exist within our society.

Anonymous white person #3 (38-year-old year old male): White privilege does exist in America. I guess with African-American people being something like 400 years behind in every social and economic area, white people are going to be born with an advantage. There are some white people that are born, and they are socially and economically behind other whites, but I think they decided to live that way or the poor choices of those before them put them at a disadvantage.

What is your overall perception of black people in America?

Anonymous white person #1: I think African American people are angry all the time, especially the women. I don't understand being unhappy all the time and always ready to fight. I also feel as if I have to prove that I am not racist with black people I work with or meet. Black people are so judgmental of one another. I see African American people hurt one another more than help one another. It is almost like they hate each other. As a teacher, I understand the history of black people in America, and I don't understand how black parents allow their children to judge others by their differences, instead of embracing differences. It seems to be so ignorant to me.

Anonymous white person #2: Black people are smart but do not use their smarts to progress themselves or their community. I see how black people can be called ignorant, but I don't believe they don't have the knowledge, I personally feel as if they just don't care to use what they learn. I know progressive black people and they seem to frown upon those that are not on their level, whether it is education, title or job status, they are quick to belittle one another. I see black people as materialistic and live for today. They don't worry about saving for the future or even for the future of their families. It seems so selfish and self-centered.

Anonymous white person #3: To be honest I see black people as animalistic. When something happens they don't like, they will destroy their own communities and each other. I know as a fact in the inner cities, black people are killing each other. I do not see them helping one another; I see a lot of backstabbing and destruction. Blacks do not care to vote and control their own communities, but they will complain about everything. Even in my company, when one black person promotes up, they will promote a white person before they a black person. I have been with my company for 15 years and when a black person promotes, we (whites) will bet each other that the black promoted will not help another black person.

The future state of black people in America

Anonymous white person #1: I see black people coming together again, if they get a leader who will lead them such as a modern Martin Luther King. I have many black friends, and I know that their spirit is strong and tenacious. If they could see how destructive, they are right now, stop killing each other, I think there is hope for this race in America. Life is what you make it and even with adversity, many black people have emerged on top in America. When I look at the Oprah Winfrey's, Tyler Perry's and others that have made something out of nothing, I still see hope.

Anonymous white person #2: If the mentality of black people does not change, they will kill each other and keep each other down. I see dysfunction in every race; I just see the dysfunction in blacks as destructive for their future generations. Let go of the anger and become progressive with self and with your community. Don't stay mad, just do something with what your ancestors have done to progress the black community.

Anonymous white person #3: To be honest, I do not see a future for this race. Either they will kill each other, or destroy each other. They do not plan ahead so they will just keep flying by the seat of their pants in life. I see self-genocide for black people.

It was truly humbling and heart wrenching to hear how the anonymous white individuals, who were brave enough to speak freely see in MY people. I left the interviews with a heavy heart but a determined spirit. It is time to heal, stop pointing fingers and be totally honest with the state of black America today. How are we helping to shape the future of our communities? I stated earlier in this chapter that we were as strong as our weakest link. So if some of us make it to "success" (whatever that looks like to you), how are we assisting in the progression of the communities we left behind? I know there are many, many people in America that start social programs in low-income communities, begin and run sports programs and volunteer their time to give back to the community. This is not to take away from those that sincerely try to progress themselves and others. There are so many people in the black community doing great things, and it is sad that we do not hear of the many wonderful things coming out of black communities more. There are so many ways where the perception of blacks and their image can be changed in media, in print and on television, however, this is not the platform to voice these ways, so I will leave this chapter where it is and end on this note. My Mother used to tell me "if one person calls you a duck do not worry about it, but if two or three people call you a duck, check your behind for feathers." Although we shouldn't move by other people's perceptions, when black-and-white people are speaking in unison, on the same subjects, it is time for a revolution.

Words taken right out of social media threads with comments about black people from black people *(2014)*

(This is in no way put here to invite violence or hate, instead to spark an interest in changing the perception from within).

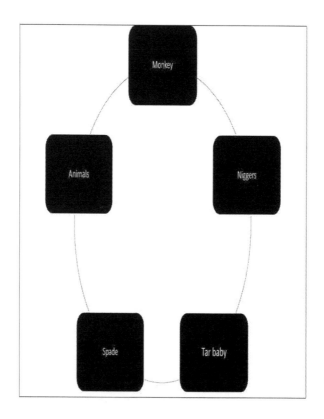

Chapter 3: Know Your Rights

"Being ignorant is not so much a shame, as being unwilling to learn" Benjamin Franklin

The purpose of this section is to discuss certain rights as it may occur when interacting with police officers. This chapter is not an exclusive list of all rights under the law, just a select few. The laws that govern our society derive from cases that made it to the United States Supreme Court, and Supreme Court Judges interpret the Constitution pertaining to the particular right in question, which then establishes case laws.

There are some basic rights that everyone should know.

1. You have the right to refuse consent to a search of your vehicle, your home and your person. (This changes if there is a warrant).

2. You have the right to be silent, if you want to exercise this right, make it verbally clear to the officer.

3. You have the right to gain Counsel (a lawyer) if you feel the need. If you cannot afford one, the courts can assign a public defender to assist you.

4. If you are not under arrest, you have the right to walk away calmly.

The above-mentioned rights are for every person, in every state and come from the Constitution of the United States.

Across the country, hundreds of thousands of officers take an oath in order to take on the role of protector, law upholder, and peacemaker. The question then becomes why there is such discontent over the actions of officers across the nation? Most of the issues between our communities and the police today come from ignorance. In no uncertain terms, am I meaning the word ignorance in a derogatory manner. The definition of ignorance is the lack of knowledge. It is amazing just how many people say that their rights have been violated after an interaction with a police officer, but when you ask them what their rights are, they cannot tell you. I think it is one of those things that don't seem to matter unless an individual feels wronged.

The United States Constitution was established in America's national government and guarantees certain basic rights for its civilians. The Constitution was signed on September 17, 1787 by 39 out of 55 delegates who attended the Constitutional convention sessions. The all-male white delegates ranged from 26 to 81 years of age. The Constitution, which contains seven articles, will not be addressed here; however, nine of the amendments in which there are twenty seven total will be addressed. The amendments which most civilians refer to as being violated when it comes to local police will be stated here.

Amendment I (1): Congress shall make no law respecting an establishment of religion, or prohibiting the free exercise thereof; or abridging the freedom of speech, or of the press; or the right of the people peaceable to assemble, and to petition the Government for a redress of grievances.

Overview of the First Amendment: This amendment protects the freedom of religion and the freedom of expression from government interference. The Supreme Court interprets the extent under the protection as applying to the entire federal government, although it is only expressly applicable to Congress. The court has also interpreted the due-process clause of the Fourteenth Amendment as protecting the rights in the first amendment from interference by state government (Fourteenth Amendment will be discussed later in this chapter). The most basic component of freedom of expression is the right to free speech. This right allows individuals to express themselves without interference or constraint by the government. The Supreme Court requires the government to provide substantial justification for interfering with the right of free speech. Government may prohibit some speech that may cause a breach of the peace or cause violence according to the Supreme Court.

Speech is unprotected if words used results in presenting a clear and present danger (Schenck v. United States, 249 US 47 1919). Fighting words is unprotected; words which would likely make a person they address commit an act of violence (Chaplinsky v New Hampshire

315 U.S. 568 1942). Obscenity is a category of speech that is unprotected by the First Amendment. Legal definition of obscenity has been difficult to establish; however, key component of obscenity is evaluated by federal and state courts using a standard established by Miller v. California 413 U.S. 19 1973. Some other cases referenced for obscenity are Roth v. United States 354 U.S. 476 1957, Reno v. American Civil Liberties Union 521 U.S. 844 (ACLU I, which addressed obscenity in the field of media). The Child Online Protection Act (COPA), Ashcroft v. Civil Liberties Union (00-1293) 535 U.S. 564 (2002) 217 F.3d 162 ("ACLU II"), and ACLU v. Mukasey, No. 07-2539 (3d Cir. July 22, 2008) are also cases which address obscenity.

So what does this entire section mean in everyday language? In essence, what the Supreme Court has said is that people have the right to assemble for peaceful and lawful purposes. People have a right to freedom of speech, however, fighting words that present a clear and present danger, and obscene words are not protected under the amendment. Freedom of press is not very different from the right to freedom of speech; it just allows an individual

49

to express themselves through publication and dissemination. The right to petition the government for a redress of grievances allows people the right to ask the government to provide relief for a wrong through the courts or other governmental action. This right work alongside the right of assembly by allowing people to join and seek change from the government.

Amendment II (2): A well-regulated Militia, being necessary to the security of a Free State, the right of the people to keep and bear Arms, shall not be infringed.

Overview of the Second Amendment: modern time's interpretation of this amendment can be confusing. The United States Supreme Court has interpreted the amendment to mean that most Americans have a constitutional right to defend themselves and their property, with force when and if necessary. In 2008 and 2010 the Supreme Court ruled that the militia reference doesn't limit arms to only military and law enforcement, but most Americans have a constitutional right to own guns for self-defense or certain legal activities such as target practice and hunting.

Not all Americans have the right to bear arms according to the Supreme Court. For example, convicted felons lose their Second Amendment rights. Also individuals who are diagnosed and certifiably mentally ill cannot bear arms.

There is the Bill of Rights that grants state and local governments the freedom to set their own laws without the interference from federal government; however, this does not mean states can override civilians' constitutional rights. The amendment allows a citizen to go hunting, but that does not mean you can hunt anywhere or anytime; local gun control rules have to be followed. Each state has separate gun control laws. If advice is needed in this area, a local civil rights attorney can assist with this complicated amendment.

The Fourth Amendment is probably the most quoted amendment when dealing with law enforcement in the United States. Law enforcement officers are taught this in great detail, and civilians should know this amendment and understand how individual cases are affected by this amendment.

Amendment IV (4): The right of the people to be secure in their persons, houses, papers, and effects, against unreasonable searches and seizures, shall not be violated, and no Warrants shall issue, but upon probable cause, supported by oath or affirmation, and particularly describing the place to be searched, and the persons or things to be seized.

Overview of the Fourth Amendment: this amendment is broken down into sections for clarity purposes. Protection from unreasonable searches and seizures by the government also includes the work done by law enforcement. This amendment is not a guarantee against all searches and seizures, but only those that are deemed unreasonable under the law.

Home: Searches and seizures inside a home without a warrant are presumptively unreasonable. The United States Supreme Court has found exceptions to this law, whereas searches without a warrant can be lawful.

A. If an officer is given consent to search (must be someone with the authority to give such consent (Payton v. New York, 445 U.S. 573, 1980).

B. If the search is incident to a lawful arrest. When the arrest is lawful, a search may be made of the person under arrest and secondly a search of the area within the control of the arrestee can be searched (United States v. Robinson, 414 U.S. 218, 1973).

C. If there is probable cause to search and exigent circumstances exist. Exigent circumstance is an emergency situation requiring quick action to prevent danger to life or serious damage to property (Payton v. New York, 445 U.S. 573, 1980).

D. If the items are in plain view. Items can include illegal substances in home that can be plainly viewed without entering the premise (Maryland v. Macon, 472 U.S. 463, 1985).

Person: When an officer observes conduct that is considered unusual and leads the officer to reasonably conclude that criminal activity may be afoot, the officer may briefly stop the suspicious person and make reasonable inquiries to confirm or dispel the officer's suspicions (Terry v. Ohio, 392 U.S. 1, 1968 & Minnesota v. Dickerson, 508 U.S. 366, 1993).

Schools: School officials need to obtain a warrant before searching a student who is under their authority; rather, a search of a student needs only to be reasonable under all circumstances.

Cars: The following list is not in its entirety, I just added the most common interaction with law enforcement and vehicles.

A. When an officer has probable cause to believe that a vehicle may contain evidence of criminal activity, they may lawfully search any area in the vehicle in which the evidence may be found (Arizona v. Gant, 129 S. Ct. 1710, 2009).

B. When an officer has a reasonable suspicion that a traffic violation has occurred or if a criminal activity is afoot, an officer may conduct a traffic stop (Berekmer v. McCarty, 468 U.S. 420, 1984 & United States v. Arvizu, 534 U.S. 266, 2002).

C. During a lawful traffic stop, an officer may conduct a pat down of the driver and passengers; the officers need not to believe that any occupant of the vehicle is involved in a criminal activity (Arizona v. Johnson, 555 U.S. 323, 2009).

D. When a valid traffic stop is conducted, the use of a narcotics detection dog that walks around the exterior of a car does not require reasonable, explainable suspicion (Illinois v. Cabales, 543 U.S. 405, 2005).

E. A state may use highway sobriety checkpoints for combating drunk driving (Michigan Dept. of State Police v. Sitz, 496 U.S. 444, 1990).

F. A state may not use a highway checkpoint program whose purpose is the discovery and interdiction of illegal narcotics (City of Indianapolis v. Edmond, 531 U.S. 32, 2000).

G. A state may set up highway checkpoints where the stops are brief and seek voluntary cooperation in the investigation of a recent crime that has occurred on that highway (Illinois v. Lidster, 540 U.S. 419, 2004).

Amendment V (5): No person shall be held to answer for a capital, or otherwise infamous crime, unless on a presentment or indictment of a grand jury, except in cases arising in the land or naval forces, or in the militia, when in actual service in time of War or public danger; nor shall any person be subject for the same offence to be twice put in jeopardy of life or limb; nor shall be compelled in any criminal case to be a witness against himself, nor be deprived of life, liberty, or property, without due process of law; nor shall private property be taken for public use, without just compensation.

Overview of the Fifth Amendment: Indictment is decided by a grand jury (usually 16 to 23 people), and a Prosecutor presents evidence to the jury usually in serious felonies in the federal legal system. Some examples of serious felonies include such crimes as murder, and attempt murder. In the case of double jeopardy, it is aimed to protect an individual from harassment through successive prosecutions of the same alleged act. This ensures the

56

significance of an acquittal as well as prevents the state from putting psychological, physical, financial and emotional troubles on the defendant. The Fifth Amendment protects defendants from having to testify if they may incriminate themselves through testimony. The Supreme Court extended the Fifth Amendment protection to encompass any situation that involves personal freedom. From this amendment came the Miranda Rights, which is the rights a police officer will inform you of. These rights include the right to remain silent, the right to have an attorney present during questioning, and the right to have an appointed attorney if the suspect cannot afford one. Due Process Clause requires the government to respect all rights and protections afforded by the Constitution before the government can deprive a person of liberty, life, or property. The Fifth Amendment only applies to the federal government, but the Fourteenth Amendment applies this due process to the states.

Amendment VI (6): In all criminal prosecutions, the accused shall enjoy the right to a speedy and public trial, by an impartial jury of the state and district wherein the crime shall have been committed, which district shall have been previously ascertained by law, and to be informed of the nature and cause of the accusation; to be confronted with the witnesses against him; to have compulsory process for obtaining witnesses in his favor, and to have the Assistance of Counsel for his defense.

Overview of the Sixth Amendment: this amendment is pretty straight forward. One thing that is important to understand is a speedy trial means reasonable timing according to multiple factors, which include allowing for Court calendar availability, prosecutor and defense attorney availability, time to select a Jury or Grand Jury and other factors.

Amendment VII (7): In suits at common law, where the value in controversy shall exceed twenty dollars, the right of trial by jury shall be preserved, and no fact tried by a jury, shall be otherwise reexamined in any Court of the United States, than according to the rules of the common law.

Overview of the Seventh Amendment: This amendment applies only to civil cases heard in federal courts. This does not involve criminal matters. It is a dispute between private parties or between a private party and the government. The right to a trial by jury is guaranteed in any civil case if the amount of money involved in the case exceeds $20. This right can be waived if both parties agree to a bench trial, which is a trial by a Judge.

Amendment VIII (8): Excessive bail shall not be required, nor excessive fines imposed, nor cruel and unusual punishments inflicted.

Overview of the Eighth Amendment: For the purpose of this book, I am only explaining the factors Courts use in order to set bail. 1. The seriousness of the offense 2. The weight or amount of evidence against the accused. 3. The extent of any ties, such as employment, family that the accused has to the community where they will be prosecuted. 4. The ability to pay a given amount. 5. The likelihood that the accused will flee the jurisdiction if released.

Amendment XIV Section 1 (14): All persons born or naturalized in the United States, and subject to the jurisdiction thereof, are civilians of the United States and of the state wherein they reside. No state shall make or enforce any law, which shall abridge the privileges or immunities of civilians of the United States; nor shall any state deprive any person of life, liberty, or property, without due process of law; nor deny to any person within its jurisdiction the equal protection under the laws.

Overview of the fourteenth Amendment: There are five sections for this Amendment; however, the only one presented here is section 1. This amendment which includes equal protection under the laws' clause, limits the ability of states to discriminate against people based upon their gender, race, and national origin. This amendment has been used to guarantee voting rights, the rights of women and minorities, school integration, and equal employment opportunities. The history of litigation under the equal protection clause mirrors the struggle for civil rights for all Americans. This amendment also allows grand jury on the state level.

Amendment XV (15): The right of civilians of the United States to vote shall not be denied or abridged by the United States or by any state on account of race, color, or previous condition of servitude.

Overview of the Fifteenth Amendment: this amendment is self-explanatory; however, I felt the need to remind people that a lot of change comes from this Amendment. Voting should never be an option but a necessity.

The above amendments were incorporated to provide a foundation of knowledge as to how the laws of our states come into existence. The Constitution lays the ground work which is later interpreted and debated in the judicial system for further clarity and resolution on cases that challenge state and federal laws as it relates to the rights of the people and government within the United States. As stated previously in the chapter, not all the amendments were touched on in this book, however, I encourage you the reader to read the Constitution and become familiar with case laws that have set standards for the United States of America. Six out of ten of the first amendments were included within this chapter. The first ten amendments make up this country's Bill of Rights.

Understanding the Constitution with its Articles, the Bill of Rights and the remaining amendments is vital to understand the performance of police officers across this country. Officers are sworn to an Oath of Office and are subject to departmental, city, state and federal regulations during the course of their daily duties. This chapter is not an exclusive list of what laws and rule's officers have to abide by. It is the foundation of police work. Take the time to understand your county, city and state laws in order to get an overarching framework as to how and why your police departments make some of the decisions as it relates to the execution of police duties.

.

Chapter 4: We Are Family

"Family is not only the biological thread that binds us, but can also be a stated mutual acceptance" Dr. Dani Lee Harris

According to an online dictionary reference, family is described as a single word with many meanings, with one definition stating, it is a group consisting of parents and children living together in a household; all the descendants of a common ancestor. Family is considered so much more than this definition. What is made clear is the individual considered to be a part of the family are important members of a larger structure; this structure also describes the fraternal order of Police, or the family of police. Entering into an academy class, everyone in training is considered a recruit, and everyone is getting to know one another and the staff that are in charge of training officers for the job. The class is treated as one, if one person messes up; the entire class is punished collectively. The individual lives, different backgrounds, ethnicity, religious beliefs, socioeconomic status, personality traits and any other difference that can be named take a back seat to the para-militant environment that each person must get acquainted with. From the onset of training, the members of a class are developing a family type bond with one another, whether it is recognized early on or not.

In the beginning, there is an atmosphere of weeding out those that may be physically and mentally weak. There are hours of physical training, pushing one's body to unthinkable measures. Physical training consists of boxing, wrestling, jumping jacks, running, obstacle courses, mountain climbing, push-ups, lean and rest (holding one's body weight up in the top push-up position for extended amounts of time) and many other positions and tasks. The physical aspect of training is very important for being able to handle oneself while on the street and is an essential part of the job. What is quickly learned in the academy is that the whole is as good as the weakest link. So when a classmate is lagging, a camaraderie spirit is quickly adapted. There are often screams from the side line of "come on," "you can do it," "don't give up," "let's go." It becomes important to the class to make sure that everyone else completes the assigned task. Self, quickly takes a back seat to "us" and "we." Terms like "there is no I in we" becomes the class motto. Month after month, week after week, day after day and hour after hour, the class that came in as individuals becomes family.

Let's look at other types of family structures that our American culture has. Some may be more welcoming in society than others, none the less, for painting the picture of family; it is important to mention them. Gangs are not necessarily classified by one specific definition, for state and local jurisdictions usually adopt their own definitions. What is noticeably missing in any definition of gangs found, is the word Family. The reason I bring this up is because of the following. I personally asked three individuals who have been known to be associated with a gang at some point in their lives, what they consider themselves. All three of them defined their "organization" as a family. I may not personally agree with what the ultimate goal or reasoning of the existence of a gang is, but what is clear is what they mean by family. Gang members speak of other gang members as family, one former gang member states "when I didn't have anything, or anyone, these people held me down; they had my back like no other; I ate when they were around, if I waited on my real fam, I would have starved." So they sought this type of structure outside of their blood lines. They speak of watching out for one another and making sure that basic needs are met like food, shelter and protection.

Sororities and fraternities also follow the family structure. The word sorority derives from the Latin word Soror, which means sister. The word fraternity derives from the Latin word Frater, which means brother. Both, meanings point back to what our society understands to be the family structure. There could be multiple chapters of a sorority or fraternity from various learning institutions, in different states, all of whom would consider someone they have never met before, but carry the same Greek letters as their brother or sister. I was told that these "family members" look out for one another, when it comes to getting an edge on obtaining employment, promotional opportunities and even assistance when helping their members in times of need. "My sisters are my family; because of them, I am where I am today...successful" (anonymous sorority member). Fraternities and sororities are also known to hold charitable events and community service events for neighborhoods. All things are done in the name and spirit of family. "When I left for school, joining a fraternity became my extended family, one in which I hold near and dear many years after leaving school" (anonymous fraternity member).

Church entities, social clubs and professional groups all consider themselves a part of a family. When I moved to the Atlanta area in 2003, I was introduced to a family entity that I was not familiar with previously. It was the "gay family" structure. It is a group of people that belong to the LGBTI (Lesbian, gay, bi-sexual, transgender, and Intersex) community that structure themselves just like the traditional sense of the word family. There is a mother, father, children, aunts, uncles, etc. The difference in this type of family unit is the fact that a "father" may be a woman or a "mother" may be a man. Since it was not something, I was familiar with, it took some time for me to get used to the idea and accept the fact that families are made up of many structures and just because they are different than what I am used to, there was no room for me to be judgmental. Different, does not necessarily mean wrong, it is just different from what one may be accustomed to and any open-minded person should be able to look at differences without judgment.

Just like the family each of us is born into; police have no control over who is or will be a part of their family. When an officer see's someone in a law enforcement uniform, acknowledgment is usually made because officers understand they are all a part of the same family. There are many reasons people decide to become officers and join this unique fraternity of brother and sisterhood. Most officers join the force because they truly want to partake in positive change, and want to serve others. There are "family officers," these are the men and woman of law enforcement that joined, following the footsteps of an influential family member, such as mom, dad, brother, etc. There is the "military officer," since police is a paramilitary (an organization similar to military force) profession, many armed force personnel find the police culture familiar to what they are accustomed to and make policing a career. Now it is not a secret, there are officers who join because they are attracted to the power that comes with being an officer. Gaining a badge, a gun, training, and the ability to take away someone's freedom is a powerful force that cannot be ignored. Among ourselves, officers refer to the last type of officer as the "bullied in "school officer." Then, like any other profession, there are the individuals who entered into the field simply because they were in need of a job, had a clean background, were in decent health and were almost certain to pass the steps to get the job. With all the various reasons why people become a part of this family; it is important to understand that there will always be different dynamics, energies, attitudes and personalities behind the police shield.

One thing to take into account is that this family, made up of different people, from various walks of life, with opposing religious and non-religious beliefs, morals and value systems, and different social and economic statuses are all brought together to be trained in a uniformed manner to protect and defend the constitutional rights of people. To protect people, and property from ill will, to minimize crime and create safe communities, to preserve the peace and public safety through the enforcement of local, federal, and state laws.

Along with duties in which each officer swears to uphold, there are some "unwritten" risks that accompany this position. Every single day, when an officer suits up (put on their uniform) they understand that they are going to work with a day filled with unknown events and situations, all which comes with the risk that they may not return home. Each officer is "silently," telling their families that they may not come home. When a person decides to join the police family, they are taking on dangers such as going towards gun shots while everyone else runs away. Dealing with car accidents, suicide, domestic calls, traffic stops, fugitives, and countless number of different calls that come through 911 dispatchers. The responsibility of an officer is enormous, there is mental, physical and emotional strain.

There are many types of family structures one can belong to. There is the biological structure, the professional structure, the church structure or simply a family created by someone for their personal reasons. No matter which structure one belongs to, family comes with its share of good, bad, and ugly. The police structure is a collective group of individuals with different personalities, objectives, and backgrounds all whom took an oath to protect the civilians and property of the United States. With the diverse background of all the individuals who join the police family, it will be a family structure with flaws, problems and challenges, similar to that of a traditional family structure. An important step to understanding is to be able to relate. This is the reason for this section and explanation of the police family. Most people can relate to the overall family structure, whether a comparison is being made to a biological family or one that has been developed.

The Patrol

There comes a time when the recruits (police in training) get through all of their physical and classroom training and are introduced to field training, the life of an officer on the streets. This is when the recruit becomes a rookie officer, one ready to take to the streets. So the rookie officer's leaves the familiarity of the classroom and the controlled environment and also the classmates they now consider their "class family" to apply all that was learned to the real-life scenarios. Not all, but most officers are nervous, yet excited to do their jobs the "text book" way. Willing to apply all that was learned in training to each new scenario. Always remembering to be safe, serve and protect people and property, this includes patrolling areas in which they are assigned, uphold and enforce laws, make arrest, issue citations and testify in court when needed. Listed is the overall meaning of a Police Officers job, but it is not exclusive to this list.

The other officers on your watch, your training officers, supervisors, and the command staff and anyone else that works with you on your shift, in your section, zone or precincts are added to your family. Answering calls come with a lot of risks, at times an officer can handle a call on their own, and other times backup officers may be requested. Domestic and traffic calls are two of the most dangerous calls an officer can go on. No two days on the job are alike, but one thing for sure is that an officer has a lot of decision making to do throughout a shift. When a call goes awry an officer may find themselves in a disagreement, scuffle or an all-out fight for one's life. When this happens, officers rely upon their "family" to come through for them. There are times when an officers life depends upon the response of others in their area to give assistance and help get control of a situation. It is in times like this that the feeling of family is strong. When officers go home and know that it was the assistance of their brother and sisters behind the shield that enabled them to get home to their blood family, which strengthen the bonds of the police family.

One call I was on involved a man who was under the influence of a narcotic (this was learned later), it took six police officers to subdue this man. He was irate swinging a broken glass bottle wildly, and committed theft from a local store. Collectively, we used our mace, our metal A.S.P. batons to try to subdue this man. The tools on our belt were non-effective in gaining control of our suspect. I arrived on the call later than the other officers and observed the officers struggling with the suspect. I ran across the street with much force and tackled the suspect to the ground. I was on top of the suspect and the other officers on the scene, jumped on my back to keep the man down. The suspect waved his hands and jumped to his feet pushing us off him as if we were light as feathers. We were in for a long fight with this suspect. One officer called for more reinforcements and the shift Sergeant, and another officer arrived on the scene. The officer who arrived with the Sergeant walked over to the suspect and sat on his back, allowing us the opportunity to get the suspects' arms behind his back in order to place the handcuffs on him. The reason I recall this story is because, the joint efforts from all the officers and the feeling of family was such a strong presence for me in this particular situation. We worked together to get the suspect under arrest, and we were in sync with wanting to make sure all the officers made it home after the shift. I broke my thumb in the scuffle and my "family" stayed with me at the hospital and made sure I made it home. That is what family does for one another.

Day in and day out, officers are working areas, beats, zones, streets and highways in order to uphold their duties and adhere to the promises they swore to when taking the police officers oath. When someone is *born* into a family, there is no oath of office, no I promise to…, no, I will upholds…, it simply means that you are a part of a family that is bonded by blood and family politics will take root as you grow up within that family. Every police officer in the United States takes an oath that guides their duties and bonds them into the police family. The following are examples of the oaths sworn to when becoming police officers.

California's oath of office general statement;
SEC. 3. Members of the Legislature, and all public officers and employees, executive, legislative, and judicial, except such inferior officers and employees as may be by law exempted, shall, before they enter upon the duties of their respective offices, take and subscribe the following oath or affirmation:

"I, _____, do solemnly swear (or affirm) that I will support and defend the Constitution of the United States and the Constitution of the State of California against all enemies, foreign and domestic; that I will bear true faith and allegiance to the

Constitution of the United States and the Constitution of the State of California; that I take this obligation freely, without any mental reservation or purpose of evasion; and that I will well and faithfully discharge the duties upon which I am about to enter.

"And I do further swear (or affirm) that I do not advocate, nor am I a member of any party or organization, political or other- wise, that now advocates the overthrow of the Government of the United States or of the State of California by force or violence or other unlawful means; that within the five years immediately preceding the taking of this oath (or affirmation) I have not been a member of any party or organization, political or other-wise, that advocated the overthrow of the Government of the United States or of the State of California by force or violence or other unlawful means except as follows:

(If no affiliations, write in the words "No Exceptions") and that during such time as I hold the office of

---

I will not advocate nor become (name of office) a member

of any party or organization, political or otherwise that advocates the overthrow of the Government of the United States or of the State of California by force or violence or other unlawful means."

And no other oath, declaration, or test, shall be required as a qualification for any public office or employment. "Public officer and employee" includes every officer and employee of the State, including the University of California, every county, city, district, and authority, including any department, division, bureau, board, commission, agency, or instrumentality of any of the foregoing. (http://www.leginfo.ca.gov/.const/.article_20)

New York's oath of office general statement;

Section 1. Members of the legislature, and all officers, executive and judicial, except such inferior officers as shall be by law exempted, shall, before they enter on the duties of their respective officers, take and subscribe the following oath or affirmation: "I do solemnly swear (or affirm) that I will support the Constitution of the United States, and the Constitution of the State of New York, and that I will faithfully discharge the duties of the office of ...., according to the best of my ability and no other oath, declaration or test shall be required as a qualification for any office of public trust, except that any committee of a political party may, by rule, provide for equal representation of the sexes on any committee, and a state convention of a political party, at which candidates for public office are nominated, may by rule, provide for equal representation of the sexes on any committee of such party (http://www.dos.ny.gov/corps/oath.html).

Atlanta's oath of office general statement; the police chief or the chief's designee is authorized, in accordance with Georgia law, to administer the oath of office to all sworn police officers employed by the City of Atlanta. When taken, the officer shall sign the official oath and copies thereof shall be filed with the Fulton County Probate Court and in the personnel records of the officer so sworn. That oath shall take the following form:

I, _____, do solemnly swear (or affirm) that I am duly qualified, according to the Constitution and laws of Georgia, to perform the duties imposed upon me as a Police Officer of the City of Atlanta, Georgia, and that I will, to the best of my ability, discharge the duties thereof, and preserve, protect, and defend the Constitution of the United States of America and the Constitution of the State of Georgia.

I swear that I am not the holder of any office of trust under the government of the United States, any other state, or any foreign state which I am prohibited from holding by the laws of the State of Georgia, nor am I the holder of any unaccounted for public money due this state or any political subdivision or authority thereof. I further swear that I will enforce the criminal laws of the State of Georgia and the ordinances of the City of Atlanta, abide by the rules and standard operating procedures governing the Atlanta Police Department, adhere to the Law Enforcement Code of Ethics published by the International Association of Chiefs of Police, and uphold the Ethics Code of the City of Atlanta. In doing so, I will be mindful of the trust that has been placed in me to improve the quality of life and make every effort to live up to that trust. I will not persecute the innocent, nor help to shield the guilty, nor will I be influenced in the discharge of my duties by fear, favor, or affection, reward, or the hope thereof. So help me God (http://atlanta.eregulations.us/code/coor_ptii_ch98_artii_div1_sec98-52).

While on patrol, officers have to know the law, understand the law and enforce the law. Understanding the different aspects of the officer's job is vital to gaining the respect of civilians. Officers on patrol are deterring crime just by being visible. How often are you driving the highways of your state, and you observe a patrol car by the side of the road? The next thing you find yourself doing is looking down at your speedometer to make sure you are not speeding. If you know you are speeding you automatically go for your breaks to come into legal compliance. How about having to break hard because the vehicle in front of you has just slammed on their breaks to come to a slow speed quickly, unnerving you because you almost slammed into the back of them. This is the power of being visible as an officer. In many situations, a person who is about to do something illegal will quickly change their mind when they see their local law enforcement man or woman in uniform patrolling the area. If an officer is called to a situation or observes someone breaking the law, it is the family of police that an officer will rely on to come to their aid if needed.

Learning how to effectively do your job and uphold the sworn oath takes classroom, field, and on-the-job training. Over time, officers develop a unique "gut feeling" that assists in their daily duties. This gut feeling is not enough alone to pull someone over, stop someone in the street or enter someone's place of residence. Reasonable Articulable Suspicion (R.A.S.) is the minimum needed for an officer to stop and question someone. R.A.S., gives officers the right to detain a suspect (briefly) for investigator purposes and may frisk the outside of a person's clothing for weapons. There has to be a set of facts or circumstances that would lead a reasonable person to believe that a suspect has, or will commit a crime. The officer uses their training and experience to articulate their beliefs. Probable cause is needed in order to take a suspicion further in an officer's investigation. Probable cause refers to the requirement in criminal law that police have a reason to arrest or search a person and to seize property as it relates to an alleged crime. Probable cause comes from the Fourth Amendment of the United States Constitution. The Amendment states "The right of the people to be secure in their person's houses, papers, and effects, against unreasonable searches and seizures, shall not be violated, and no warrants shall issue, but upon probable cause, supported by Oath or affirmation, and particularly describing the place to be searched, and the persons or things to be searched." Probable cause for an arrest without a warrant is discussed in great detail in the "know Your Rights" chapter. It is the Constitution of the United States that govern the actions of police officers, so it is very important to understand your rights under federal, state, city and county laws.

When officers sign up to be a part of the police family, there are a lot of aspects of the job they will have to learn. Taking individuals from all walks of life and training them to be fair, calm, reasonable, and righteous according to the Constitution, the federal, state and local law is challenging. The responsibility of officers is huge and should be taken into account before judgments are made. Remember that what one may see as fair and reasonable may not seem the same to another because of ethnic, religious, and social differences. Police officers are taught to put those differences aside and uniformly allow the law to dictate outcomes regardless of personal beliefs and opinions.

.

Chapter 5: The Police Structure

"You can't move forward until you look back" Cornell West.

Law Enforcement is described as individuals and agencies that are responsible for enforcing laws, this includes Federal, State, County and Sheriffs offices. Law enforcement agencies are used for the prevention, detection, and investigation of crime and the apprehension and detention of individuals suspected of violating laws. This includes titles such as Sheriff Deputies, Police Officers (both City and County), State Troopers, Peace Officers, Public-Safety Officers, Federal Bureau of Investigations (FBI), Drug Enforcement Administration (DEA) Customs Agents, and Marshals, to name the majority.

Law enforcement agencies often work with each other in order to enforce laws and bring forth justice when dealing with violations of laws. However, for this book we are discussing the local city and county police agencies. The local agencies that are responsible for the day to day interaction with the civilians of our communities within the United States. The following pages are filled with important background information about the United States police structure, the developmental process of the police communities, and how the police community grew to be where it is today.

Understanding the history of policing in the United States is crucial to see the progression over time. Policing in America followed the development of policing in England. There were two forms of policing in the early colonies. One form was referred to as the "Watch," which was informal and the second form; private-for-profit policing was known as "The Big Stick." The watch system was made up of volunteers from the community whose primary duty was to warn of impending danger. The watch system was created and ran in Boston Massachusetts. The night watch was implemented in Boston in 1636, then in New York in 1658 and in Philadelphia in 1700. The night watches were not that effective as the men would drink or sleep throughout their shift. Many of the watchmen were on punishment duty or attempting to evade military service. The day watches were formed first in Philadelphia in 1833 and in New York in 1844. Service provided by the watch system included lighting street lamps, running soup kitchens, recovering children who were lost, provided some social services and capturing animals that ran away to name a few.

The big stick, also known as constables were official law enforcement officers who received a fee for serving warrants. The constables were also used as land surveyors and other non-law enforcement functions were expected. In some cities, constables also had the responsibility of supervising the activities of night watchman. The informal modalities of policing went on well after the American Revolution. Centralized municipal police departments emerged in 1838, in the city of Boston. This is when the first police force was created. New York City followed in 1845. By the 1880s all United States major cities had a police force in place. All though the police departments operated differently in each city, there were some similar characteristics. All the departments were financially supported publicly and bureaucratic. Each department has fixed procedures and rules. All the officers hired were continuous employees. All the officers were full-time employees. The departments was held accountable by central governmental authorities. Although there were some similar characteristics, there were some differences as well. The police departments in the south followed a completely different path then their northern counterparts. The south police started with "slave patrols" in the Carolina colonies and was copied in the rest of the southern states in 1704. The functions of these slave patrols were to chase down and apprehend runaway slaves, to organize terror to deter slave revolts, and to maintain discipline for slave-workers that faced summary justice.

In the 1800's the distinct characteristic of policing in the United States was the direct reflection of political involvement. Politicians hired and retained police officers in order to keep their political power. Keeping the officer employed, the officers would encourage local civilians to vote for their employer. When politicians were voted out during this period, the entire personnel of the department would change as well. Officers in this era were equipped with a hickory club, a whistle and a key to the call box which was telephone lines linked to police headquarters (similar to calling 911 today). There was little supervision over cops of this era, which led to many incidents of police misconduct and corruption. Most of the corruption was directly related to politics and included rigging election and persuading people to vote a certain way, so that the officers could keep their jobs and the politician could hold their position.

From the 1900s through the 1970s policing in America saw a reform. The direct involvement of politics with police was viewed as a problem by public and police reformers during the mid to late 19th century. Civilians attempted to pressure police agencies to make changes, which were unsuccessful, until the early 20th century when reform efforts began to take hold. The United States police departments started to see significant changes in policing, with the help of the progressive movement. During this reform period, professionalism was brought to the police departments. Officers were better trained, the quality of offices hired was increased. New technology was implemented such as two-way radios and motorized patrol vehicles. One way politics was separated from the departments was with implementation of civil-service systems in the hiring and promotion of officers (which was seen mostly in the northern states, even today). Some forms of the civil-service systems were implemented in southern states, such as promotional systems.

During the 1950's which marked the beginning of a social movement, race relations were brought to the attention of all Americans. There were several events, which involved African American organizing civil rights marches and demonstrations across the country in the mid-1950s. Such events like the arrest of Rosa Parks, the Montgomery bus boycott, and many more caused the police reform to place efforts on responding to calls for service and managing crimes in a reactive manner. The reform took the attention away from social disorder and the quality of life of civilians in an attempt to quell the growing tension between the black community and the police.

Today we are in the community era, as we move out of the reform phase of policing in America. The community era relies heavily on a close working relationship between the police departments and the communities in which they serve. Top police executives are more involved with the concerns of the community. Today we see an increase in community meetings, town-hall meetings and events that integrate departments and civilians. This new community era calls for cooperation, understanding and a sensitivity to the community. Civilians are more empowered to voice their concerns, call for platforms in which their needs are addressed and ask for police accountability in matters that could cause social unrest.

Chapter 6: From The Mouth Of Officers

"Life is a succession of lessons which must be lived to be understood"
Ralph Waldo Emerson

The officers mentioned throughout this chapter
have been given a pseudonym to protect their identities.
The demographics of the officers are true and factual. The
reason for this has nothing to do with the officers trying to
hide. I decided to make identities anonymous in order to
provoke honesty from the officers, without any fear of
retaliation from their respective departments or
communities for voicing their thoughts and opinions. Four
black, five white, and one Hispanic officer have been
interviewed in this chapter. In total, there were eight men
and two women interviewed. Using a word of mouth
method to get involvement, these officers were willing to
share their thoughts with the world. The interviewees are
all active officers in law enforcement. The topics in which
they share their thoughts on are, profiling, training, media,
quotas, myths of police officers or police work and advice
they would share with civilians and/or officers.

Officer Baker: is a Caucasian male who works and resides in Georgia and is employed by a large Police Department (compared to other departments in the South). Officer Baker has been in law enforcement for a total of 14 years. Officer Baker was born and raised in Buffalo New York.

Profiling: Officer Baker stated, "everyone profiles, not racially but criminal behavior follows a profile that officers look for." Officer Baker explains that police are taught to look to the behavior of individuals and understand how to read body language. If there is a black or white male standing on the corner, and as soon as they spot an officer pull up in a patrol car and they take off running, experience has taught Officer Baker, that more likely than not, the individual is partaking in some criminal activity. Officer Baker goes on to express that this does not apply to every black or white male on the corner, just the majority.

Shooting: Officer Baker states, "90% of officers are not a good shot. The largest part of the body is the torso and center mass." Officer Baker goes on to say that officers are not trained to shoot arms and legs because there are no arms and legs on the targets in which officers train on.

92

Officer Baker further state that most police officers are not trained to be a marksman (someone skilled in shooting, especially with a pistol or rifle).

Traffic Stops: Officer Baker suggests that civilians comply with officer's request when being pulled over for a traffic violation. Keeping hands of everyone in the vehicle visible at all times puts the officer at ease, not relaxed just not as tensed. Officer Baker states, "stop being belligerent with officers on a traffic stop, you only make things worse." Officer Baker also wants civilians to know, that a lot of movement in the vehicle is going to make an officer nervous, so stop moving unless you are getting vehicle information and only after you were asked to retrieve such items.

Media: Officer Baker believes that media outlets are fueling the anger and resentment between police and the community with one-sided reporting. "All the good that officers do is not get played out in the media as long as the negative." Officer Baker feels that the black officers, if interviewed, would state that some of the actions taken by white officers would be similar if presented with the same situations.

Advice to Officers: Try not to go hands on (fighting suspects), use the tools of your gun belt. "In all my years of policing, I have never had a use of force compliant; I just use my tools."

Advice to Civilians: "The issues we see today are not training issues." officers can make bad decisions; however, that is an individual problem not a police problem.

Myths: The biggest myth that sticks out in Officer Baker's mind is "All officers want to put everyone in jail."

Officer Larry: Is a Caucasian male who resides and works in Georgia as a Police Officer. Officer Larry has been an officer for 20 years, who states, "I was raised helping others. I became an officer to improve people's quality of life."

Profile: Officer Larry states that he does not profile for race, for he could care less about race. "Break the law, draw attention, I will handle it accordingly." Based on his training Officer Larry states that officers learn how to observe peoples' verbal and nonverbal behavior to see if someone is breaking the law or not.

Shooting: Officer Larry states, "officers are not taught to shoot to kill, but to stop the threat." People are small moving targets, so it is easier to shoot center mass, since it is the biggest part of the body, and it just happens to be the area that stops a person from continuing with an action.

Traffic Stops: It is vital to keep hands in plain sight says Officer Larry when speaking of the subject of traffic stops. It is important to move slow and do what the officer asked of you. Being polite helps more so than being unpleasant with an officer and never argue with the police at the scene of a traffic stop. Fighting traffic infractions take place in the court room not on the side of the road.

Quotas: When discussing quotas, Officer Larry states, "Quotas are a double edge sword, technically there are no quotas, and they are illegal, but if you don't comply with a certain amount of arrest, your beat, and off days are threatened."

Myths: "All cops were bullied in High School and need power"

Media: The media is doing an awful job by trying to slaughter police as a whole. "The Ferguson case has been hyped up by the media." In Alabama, there was a black cop that shot and killed an unarmed white, naked man. The media did not give that story much attention at all. Media sells drama and as long as the public buys; they will keep selling.

Advice to civilians: "I fought a man for 5 and ½ minutes before my backup arrived, all though I did not want to think this way, I was preparing myself to take his life for he had his hand on my gun." No officer goes to work wanting to take a life, there are just so many factors that are involved with making that decision.

Officer Murray: Is a Puerto Rican male who is a 12-year veteran of a Georgia Police Department. Born and raised in Chicago, Officer Murray, wanted a change and decided to join Georgia's finest.

Profiling: Officer Murray feels profiling is a tool needed for law enforcement officers. Experience tells you that a certain person with certain characteristics is someone law enforcement will look at. Pants hanging low, hanging on a corner or in the streets with suspicious behavior will draw the attention of an officer, whether the officer is black, Hispanic or white. Profiling can also be negative if not used with experience. It is important not group a race of people together for bad or good.

Shooting: Officers are not trained to kill, but to stop the threat. To shoot someone in the arms and legs will not stop the threat.

Traffic Stops: When stopped by the police for a traffic violation, be polite and obey orders says Officer Murray. When a person has a bad attitude, it puts an officer on the defense, which could create a dangerous situation. Whether there is one person or more in a car, put your hands on the steering wheel and passengers put their hands on the dash board or the seat in front of them. Do not move around for it makes an officer nervous. If the car has dark tinted windows, if possible, roll down all the windows when there are multiple people in the car. Turn overhead or interior lights on at night helps an officer to be at ease.

Quotas: Officer Murray believes that there is an unwritten quota. In high-crime areas, it is expected to be high arrest numbers. When numbers are low, it is assumed that officers are not being productive. Something is wrong when crime goes up, but arrest does not.

Family: There was a time when the police felt like a close family, but times have changed, and it doesn't feel this way anymore.

Myth: "Cops are cocky and we all violate people's rights for no reason" Officer Murray further states "Another myth is that officers feel like they are above the law and cannot make mistakes; officers do remember they are human beings."

Officer Adam: A Caucasian female, who is a 16-year veteran of a Georgia Police Department. Born and reared in the South, Officer Adam states that she has spent 15 out of 16 years patrolling a black neighborhood.

Profiling: Officer Adam states, "working in a black neighborhood for 15 years, you learn that profiling is a part of the job." Young black males between the ages of 14 through 16 were responsible for the majority of the crime in her patrol area. So when a group of young males are hanging out loitering, it grabbed the attention of all officers. Officer Adam developed a good sense for spotting gang activity through the years of working the streets of Georgia. When observing a white person in an all-black neighborhood at a certain time of evening, her experience has taught her that most likely they are in the area to buy dope.

Shooting: If an officer has to pull out their weapon to shoot someone, it is to stop a threat. This would be a life-or-death situation that would have anyone scared; however, the officer has to protect self or others. Taking away the threat becomes the only option at that point. Worrying about liability will hit the officer later, but at that moment, the office just wants to get out of the situation alive. Signing up to be an officer comes with being willing to take a life if need be. This is a part of the job that a lot of people do not want to talk about, but is necessary to understand.

Traffic Stops: Officer Adams wants civilians to understand how important being respectful on a traffic stop is in how the officer will deal with you. Stay calm, and know that you have a right to ask why you were stopped. Being argumentative is never a good or helpful thing. It is vital to keep hands in a place that the officer can see them and don't move around too much in the vehicle for it makes most officers nervous.

Quotas: Officer Adams states officers do have quotas or better known as performance reviews. When an officer is productive on the street, they do not have to worry about losing their assignment or their days off (if they have desirable days off). It is not a time of the month thing like most people thinks. There are no quotas that need to be made by the beginning or end of each month. Presence is delegated by crime statistics, if there is a spike in crime in a particular area, more officers will be dispatched to that area. This is just common police practice. When there is a media story about quotas in the police department, performance reviews or quotas go away for a little while, and then eventually make their way back into production.

Myths: officers do not have feelings, and they often become drunks and beat up on their spouses.

Advice to civilians and Police: "Be Safe"

Officer Henry: Is a Black Male officer who has been in law enforcement as a Police Officer in Georgia for the past 10 years. Born and raised in Georgia, Officer Henry left the school system to become a Police Officer with the desire to protect and serve the communities of Georgia.

Profiling: Officer Henry believes that racial profiling happens more often than not. All officers profile to an extent for it is a part of the job. Certain vehicles, characteristics of individuals, stick out to an officer with experience. Even though officers are trained in the academy, the way in which that officer will think on the street will be molded by the field trainer and training that officer gets with on-the-job training. Each officer develops a sixth sense for the job after time and experience. Profiling is not necessarily a bad thing; it all depends on how it is used or abused.

Quotas: Quotas do exist; however, it is an imaginary policy, and nothing is in writing. An officer who is not performing the way their Chain of Command like, will be transferred, their shift switched and their days off changed. There was a written policy that would have been considered a quota but when the media requested a copy of the policy, the policy was destroyed.

Shooting: Officer Henry states, "officers are taught to stop the threat." This will not happen if limbs are shot, so center mass and head shots are taught. The training range does not have arms and legs on the target to practice on. There are only torso and head targets given for practice at firing range.

Traffic Stops: When an officer stops a vehicle at night, it is important to pull over as soon as possible, to not make the officer think you are fleeing. Pull over in a well-lit area and call 911 if you are fearful. Keep your hands on the steering wheel and put the overhead light on if possible. For vehicles with dark tint, open all the windows. Be courteous with the officer and answer questions asked. Don't try to prove your case in the street; this is what court is for. Keep hands up and visible at all times. If you or your vehicle is armed (weapon on your person or in your car) let the officer know.

Myths: Officer Henry states a big myth for him is that "officers never cross the thin blue line and will not stand up for wrong." For him, standing up for the rights of other has got him transferred five times within one year, so there are a lot of officers, who do the right thing.

Advice to civilians: Stop prejudging, judge officers by their character not their uniform. Most officers do the right thing, and sign up to protect and serve others.

Officer King: Is a Caucasian male that is employed by a west coast (Los Angeles) Police Department. Officer King has been on the force for 21 years.

Profiling: According to Officer King, profiling is simply searching for activity that does not look right or something that is out of place. A perp (short for a perpetrator) is going to act a certain way, suspicious. Experience teaches you the characteristics of a perp. Cops are not out to pinpoint a specific group of people, but instead seek behavior characteristics.

Traffic Stops: When being pulled over by an officer do not get defensive, it makes you look guilty of something. Remember that the police officers are just as nervous as you are. Allow the officer the opportunity to explain why you were stopped. Do not assume harassment is imminent when encountering an officer. Officer King admits that a person being pulled over by the police may get a rude officer at times, but it is your right to ask for their supervisor or log a complaint against the officer later. There will be officers, who will stop you for driving black, being female, etc., just play it cool and handle it later. Being rude will not get you anywhere positive in that situation.

Officer King recalls a traffic stop in which he followed a female driving 85 miles per hour in a 55 mile per hour zone for 3 miles attempting to pull her over. When the driver did pull over, she went behind a gas station and turned off her lights. Officer King approached the car, and the female driving screamed "you just stopped me because I am black." Officer King replied "no; I stopped you for driving 85 in a 55 mile per hour zone." The female driver requested Officer King Supervisor and complained about racial profiling. Officer King was on desk duty awaiting the completion of an internal affair's investigation in which he was cleared of all charges. Officer King stated, he performed his job fairly and justly, never looking at color or race in the execution of his duties.

Shooting: Officer King believes that law enforcement officials do not want to kill anyone, but if they shoot someone, it is to stop a threat. Most officers are only 80% accurate in shooting so they will target the largest part of the body which is center mass.

Quotas: Quotas do exist but the order is not written down. No matter where you work, performance is expected. In law enforcement, performance is measured by quotas. If you are being a productive officer, you will get citations and arrest during your workday. Interacting with civilians leads to arrest of major criminals in a lot of cases. If officers are not engaging the civilians, a mass murderer or a rapist may get away.

Advice to Civilians: 'Stop following leaders such as Al Sharpton, who only stirs up controversy in order to make money by playing games with the race card."

Advice to Officers: "Don't let your personal beliefs get into the way of you doing your job."

Officer Brown: Is a Black officer from New York City and has been a Police Officer for 19 years. Born and raised in New York City, Officer Brown entered the Police Department following the footsteps of his older brother who retired from Policing 10 years ago.

Profiling: Officer Brown believes that racial and criminal profiling is done every day by most officers. Profiling is a part of the job. The younger generation of officers are changing the way in which profiling is being conducted. When Officer Brown first started Policing, He believes that profiling was done more with race being a major factor, but today profiling is done more by locations and behaviors. "There will always be those officers who will pull over a person simply because of the color of their skin; however, that is not the norm." Officers go after criminals no matter

106

the ethnic background. If you have a white officer working in a black area, of course the majority, if not all of their arrest is going to be minorities. This stands true for black officers working in white areas.

Shooting: Officers are trained to stop a person from performing an act that will bring bodily harm to another person. This is done by shooting a person in the chest or head area. Police are not trained to maim and when their adrenaline is pumping the officer would not be able to aim for an arm or leg.

Quotas: Yes, they exist, but are illegal. I work for a numbers driven police department. Higher number of arrest seem to push crime statistics down and is a false front that crime is low. Quotas are an unwritten rule in most departments and come from police headquarters to the precincts across the city. Politics play a major role in quotas, in my opinion.

Traffic Stops: Make the officer feel at ease with politeness and cooperation. Do not be combative; allow your case to be heard in court. You cannot win an argument with an officer who has a ticket book in hand.

Don't get angry when you know you are in the wrong, and you did break the law. Rules of the road are made to protect everyone, including you and your family.

Myths: "Officers only want power, when indeed most officers want to help others."

Advice: "Stop believing everything the media says or hypes up."

Officer Morey: Is a Black female officer who has been in law enforcement for the last 13 years and is employed by a Georgia Police Department. Officer Morey feels as if she was born to be an officer and enjoys her job immensely.

Profiling: Officer Morey states she profiles and has to in order to stay observant performing her job duties. "If there is a white man in a black neighborhood, or vice versa, it will raise my suspicions, especially if I know the area and I know a person doesn't belong there." If an officer profiles because of race or class or any one reason other than criminal suspicion, it is wrong and that is not how that officer was trained. At times personal beliefs and bias become a part of how an officer will do their job, and this is unfortunate.

Shooting: I was trained to shoot the largest part of the body, so I don't miss. Officers are taught to stop the threat. If an officer is in a situation, their adrenaline is going, they are nervous, breathing hard, they want to be sure not to miss their target. It is really simple why we shoot the largest part of the body.

Traffic Stops: Traffic stops is one of the most dangerous things a police officer can do. There is no telling what can go wrong when approaching a vehicle. The best thing to do when you are stopped by the police is to not move a lot and keep your hands visible at all times. Be polite because it really does go a long way. Officers do not randomly pick people just to stop them for no reason. Obey the law and the chance of you getting stopped by the police is slim to none.

Quotas: "There is no such thing as quotas, my Department promotes productivity."

Advice for civilians: "This is my job and I am just like you, human."

Officer George: Is a Caucasian male who has been a Las Vegas Police Officer for the last 17 years. Office George, a Nevada native loves his job and became a police officer because he wanted an exciting career and did not want to work a 9 to 5 job.

Profiling: Officer George stated, "I am that officer who profiles; I profile black people because where I work, they seem to be the ones that break the law most often." Officer George goes on to express that he is not proud of having to profile; however, his time working the streets has taught him what to look for and how to police effectively. Officer George stated he was not implying he won't arrest a person who is white or any other ethnicity if they are breaking the law, because he would and has arrested others. When Officer George observes a group of black males in certain areas, his experience taught him that someone in that group is probably breaking the law.

Shooting: "In the event that I have to pull my weapon out, it is in a dire situation, and I am prepared to pull the trigger." No officer wants to take a life; however, every officer wants to go home to their families, so they will do what they were trained to do in order to go home.

Traffic Stops: If an officer stops you, it is most likely; you broke the law in some way. Sometimes it is not a moving violation, but you may have an equipment violation (broken/out light, no tag light, missing mirror, etc.). Just relax and be calm, the officer would like to be done with your stop just as much as you want them to leave. Being nasty will not get you very far on a traffic stop, all it does is make the officer defensive. Keep your hands where the officer can see them at all times. Just listen to the officers demands, and you will be away from the stop sooner than later.

Quotas: "I think every department has a quota, even if they do not call it that." Quotas are a way to gauge the activity of the officers. Lazy officers will not produce high numbers and the higher ups will see this by their numbers.

When the city wants to generate more revenue, they get officers to write more tickets, it is as simple as that.

Advice for Civilians: "Not all White Officers are racist"

Officer Dave: Is a black male who has been employed for the past 14 years with Washington DC Police Department. Officer Dave left the armed forces and decided to become a police officer to begin a career he thought would be exciting.

Profiling: Officer Dave believes that all officers have to profile; it is a part of the job of a good officer. The FBI profiles in order to get close to a suspect in their investigations and the same concept apply to local law enforcement officers. Profiling is only bad if you think the wrong way. Profiling just on the race of a person is not right and should not be tolerated. However, if you are patrolling a black neighborhood, and you observe a group of white college students riding through the neighborhood at 3 am, this is going to raise suspicion because they stick out.

Shooting: Officers are taught to neutralize a threat. If an officer has to pull their weapon, then imminent danger exists and someone has to be stopped immediately. No officer wants to take the life of another, but will if needed. If an officer shoots a person, the situation calls for deadly force, and this does not include shooting arms and legs. Shooting someone in their limbs does not stop a threat; only shooting center mass and head shots will stop a person. Officers are not trained to kill but to stop the threat.

Traffic Stops: Officer Dave wants civilians to understand that when a person is being stopped by the Police, you never know why you are being stopped until you are informed. Your vehicle may fit the description of a nearby bank robbery or you simply may have a light out. An officer is going to be on the edge when they approach your vehicle. Officers are trained to understand that vehicle stops are one of the most dangerous calls they can go on, so they may seem on edge at the beginning. Stay calm and be polite so that you can put the officer at ease. Don't fight the situation at the scene, stay courteous. Keep your hands on the steering wheel, and don't make sudden movements.

Follow the officer's directions and ask if you need to go in glove box or center console. Remember officers are supposed to be on the edge until they are made to feel at ease. This doesn't mean the officer will be relaxed.

Quotas: Officer Dave states that his department used to have quotas; however, they did away with it. Officer productivity is monitored and encouraged throughout the department. Officer Dave does believe that most departments do have quotas, whether written or expressed.

Myth: "Police officers used to get bullied in school."

Advice to Civilians: Understand that police officers want to protect the communities they patrol. Most officers want to help others and do well as an officer. Officers protect you from nightmares so that you don't have to experience them, even paying with their lives at times

Chapter 7: It Can Get Better (Community)

"I alone cannot change the world, but I can cast a stone across the waters to create many ripples" Mother Teresa

In this chapter, we explore some options that can be implemented to move communities in the direction of a better working relationship with law enforcement. Clearly neither the communities, nor the police departments are leaving society. Working together is the only positive option. If we can work alongside one another and build a foundation of peace, respect and understanding, this may be a great new beginning. When I speak of communities, I speak of all communities, regardless of class or race. Separating communities has been going on way too long. Working together, it really shouldn't matter the economic status, or race of a particular community. The fact of the matter is that police are employed in all facets of our society and should render the same services' period. Again, some may feel as if this does not take place, and I understand that. The great thing is with empowerment change can be demanded.

Understanding the Relationship between Voting and Law Enforcement

This book has been examining the relationship of communities and local law enforcement that most people will encounter daily. This would include your police departments and your local Sheriffs' office. Police departments are usually led by chiefs or commissioners. Chiefs and commissioners are appointed by a mayor who is an elected official. The chief/commissioner is the head of the department (the one in charge). However, the city officials (mayor) have the ultimate say in how each police department operates. This is important to understand because a mayor has a variety of subjects that are important to voters, not just the police department. So if there is a conflict between the police departments and the community, the mayor will be in the middle trying to bring peace to each side for they have a vested interest in pleasing the people that put them in office.

The sheriff, on the other hand, is the only law enforcement leader who is elected by the voters of the county. This means that the sheriff answers directly to the people who voted them into office. The only job of the sheriff is to worry about things concerning the law and order. The reason why it is so important to understand the structure of your community is to understand, who to hold accountable. When dealing with an issue with a chief, you have to remember that the chief has to answer to their boss who appointed them. When dealing with an issue with a sheriff, you can rest assured that they are thinking about the concerns of the majority who voted for them.

When going to the voting polls, know who you are voting for. It is important to see the background history of a candidate, whether it is the mayor or the sheriff. How were issues with law enforcement dealt with in the past for those that have a longer political career? If they are new to the political arena, you may not have any background in order to form an opinion. Issues and concerns of how a candidate may deal with their local law enforcement agency can always be addressed during campaign time. This is vital to putting the people in office that can lead your

117

community to better police/community relations. Complaining about the issues will not help, holding your elected officials accountable and making sure to vote officials in office that have your community concerns as priority is a good route to explore.

Law Enforcement Ride Along

Police ride along is an opportunity for civilians to ride in the patrol car with an officer for a shift. This is particularly helpful for community members who want to observe typically what an officer faces during a day. Check with your local police or sheriff departments to see if they participate in such a program. Most individuals whom I know participated in a ride along enjoyed it immensely. They gained a new profound respect for officers' job duties and were enlightened with the joys and pains of policing. Departments that do participate in the program may ask for a waiver to be signed. This is typical in order to protect the department from liability.

No two days are alike for an officer, so going for a ride along will give a civilian a better picture of police work.

When I had a civilian ride with me on a ride along, they describe the experience as fun and educational. It helps when civilians ask questions of the officer to dispel myths and learn some in depth reasons why following procedures and protocols are vital to law enforcement work. A civilian can ride for an entire shift, half a shift or whatever works for the officer and the civilian partner. Part of the issues with the community and law enforcement today is a lack of understanding. Taking the time to learn the job of an officer will enlighten most civilians and not only bring understand, but a sensitivity that cannot be fostered any other way.

Civilians Academy

Some law enforcement agencies have a citizen's academy. This is when civilians are invited into the police academies training center or some place that can accommodate officers and civilians. The mission of most civilians' academy is to educate communities with the operation of their law enforcement agency. This is also a time for the department to obtain valuable feedback from those participants on ways to enhance police/community

119

relations. The programs are out there and can be utilized by the civilians. I urge people to take advantage of such programs and get acquainted with local agencies. It is one thing to sit on the side line and complain about what is not right, but it is empowering to civilians to participate in such programs and get involved in problem solving behaviors.

Mostly at citizen's academies, different departments from within the agency will come and offer information regarding such things as department overview, use of force, identity theft, internal affairs, K9 demonstration and much more. Some agencies have the academy set for a specific time. For example, every Monday for 10 weeks from 6pm to 9pm. This is a wonderful opportunity to build a working relationship with your local agency. Civilians' academies are not intended to serve as an accredited law enforcement course but instead used as a training tool.

Community Events

Participating in events that are held by your local agency is also a great way to begin important dialogue and build social relationships with law enforcement agencies.

120

Some agencies call these settings community events; some are known as public gatherings, cultural celebrations, police celebrations and more. These events draw the community members outside for fun and celebration. With something for each age group to enjoy, this is a great way to see the people behind the badge in a different light. These gatherings are a way for members from the community to humanize their local police outside of 911 calls. Events as such, are ways in which departments try to bring the police and community together. Not to participate when the ability is there is a reflection on those that do not want to make relations better. Simply put, I recognize that there are members from the community that just want to complain and will not participate in healing, or building efforts put forth by their local agency.

Law Enforcement Career Day

This was an idea brought to me by a member of a community who thought it would be a great way to build relations with their police department. What this idea would entail is civilians coming in and tailing law enforcement for a day. A community member could tail the

Chief of Police and throughout the file and ranks of a department. So you may have someone tailing an investigator, or a beat officer, crime analysis, sergeant, lieutenant, and deputy chief etc. This is also a great way to expose the civilians to the job duties of officers in different capacities. This will allow civilians to examine what it takes for a police agency to run efficiently and effectively.

Association of Police Athletic/Activities Leagues, Inc. (PAL)

PAL programs are implemented for a variety of reasons outside of recreation. Programs like PAL identifies a lack of suitable recreational facilities and equipment for youths in a community. There may be potentially dangerous situations that exists, which may lead to juvenile crime or violence, such as poverty, low-income areas, etc. Implementing programs such as PAL help to address social issues in particular areas.

Distrust of the police is something our society deals with daily, in every facet of our communities, especially among the youths of inner-city areas. However, I recognize that a lot of programs for inner-city youths do not receive funding for many programs to survive. Police departments get funding from city, state and federal grants as well as businesses. Some local civic groups, police officers associations and service clubs may also provide funding for such a program to exist within the community. For those that may be interested in donating to their local PAL program, most if not all are 501 (c) (3) (federal tax exempt), and donations are a tax write-off for such organizations (yes, that was a plug; this program is near and dear in my heart as I have seen lives saved and transformed by PAL).

Some programs that youths participate in are as follows; baseball, boxing, football, Judo, track, tennis basketball, cooking lessons, tutoring in all educational areas, and much more. The programs vary by location, so contact your local police agency to enquire more. Programs such as PAL have statistically proven to help relations between police and youths as well as provide youths with alternative life choices leading them to become productive civilians of society.

Chapter 8: How Police Departments Can Help Make Things Better

"I am in favor of community policing because it builds better working relationships with the communities" Vincent Frank

Increase Moral

It really isn't as complicated as it may seem to raise moral within police departments. The fastest way to increase morale, is to put people where they will be happiest or close to it. Most times, officers come out of the academy, go on patrol and stay on the beat working day in and day out. The officers are either waiting for an opportunity to promote or simply stay on patrol, enjoying their days off and shift. When officers interview for the job, there is a section that asks about education, hobbies and interest. If this section were evaluated ever so often, the department will discover hidden talents that could progress their departments. There are officers who are good with statistics (crime analysis), chess (strategic planning), speakers (public affairs), English (report writing), marksmanship (swat, or sniper), teachers (academy

124

instructors), and this is just to name a few. Nepotism is a real issue in every facet of society, the last place it should be is in law enforcement. Just because I know or I am related to Joe Blow, doesn't make me qualified for everything. Again putting people where they would be happiest (without nepotism) even if it is part time is a great way to move a department's moral in the upswing.

One-Person vs. Two-Person Patrol Units

Studies have been done on the effectiveness of two-person patrol units, and this is really a topic that should be explored and even tested in all departments. I will just point out some pros for two-person patrols. Two officers' on patrol increase's observation during interrogations. Furthermore it allows for better community interaction when two officers answer calls. Calls such as domestic, usually have multiple cars sent to answer, two-person patrols leaves other units available for other matters. Much more territory can be covered with two-person patrols, it is difficult to drive a vehicle, look out for suspects, and observe their surroundings. Two people can better handle conflict on a scene without having to dispatch multiple vehicles. The reason this section is important is for the reader to understand some of the stress that go into daily patrols that tends to push officers away from "community policing" and instead have them "humping 911 calls" (jumping from call to call). The perception given is that the officer does not care about the call; they are not interested in helping and often seem distracted. Two-person patrols would help in community perception.

10 Hours Shifts for Law Enforcement

Ok, you are probably asking yourself what in the world does 10-hour shift have to do with better relations between law enforcement and communities. Well, I will list some results from studies to show how this helps the officers and the communities. Would you agree that an officer that have higher moral would do better with community relations? Well if you said yes, you are in line with what the studies show. Officers who works ten-hour shifts are more rested, have higher quality of work life, higher moral and could potentially have overall better health. 10-hour shifts allows more overlapping officers in the streets at critical times for crime-fighting measures. This is also important when it comes to cost-saving measures for local departments. Saving money in one area can allow money to be allocated to better training for officers. Simply stated, happier, and healthier police officers help to foster positive community relations.

Open Up Communications

It is difficult to fix problems, when problems are not stated. Opening up communication between communities and law enforcement can help. Having communities and police leaders meet for a period of time to improve relations between residents and law enforcements has been helpful across the nation. This really should take place in every community where there is tension. Bringing leadership together is a start; however, the communication efforts should eventually be brought to the broader community. Again, complaining and reiterating the problems will not solve anything. Bringing solutions and implementing new initiatives for police and community efforts will yield positive results. Implementing a liaison officer who resembles the community in which they represent also opens up communication. Having this liaison officer work among the members from the community, there will be a pulse integrated among the civilians which will benefit both local leaders and police departments. This would not be a means to provide everything the community wants and asks for, it is simply a way to get concerns heard quickly and brought to the right people in the department that can address these concerns.

Taking Political Agenda off The Table

Anyone who has been associated with law enforcement for any length of time, understand how political agendas can easily overshadow the needs of both the department and the community. It is imperative that programs, police training and community empowerment stand the test of time, if things are to get better. Politicians should be concerned with diversifying their departments to mirror the community in which the officers serve. There are studies that proves this helps with relations between communities and the police. Instead of just listening to what the majority of non-law enforcement members says. For example, implementing body cameras, why are there not test done before decisions are made? Too many times decisions and

128

promises are made for the community before consultation takes place. Holding police officers responsible does not have anything to do with suiting them up with body cameras, where in the event of a fight or scuffle, none of the event will be captured. In order to hold people accountable, you have to train them better, inform them more, integrate them in the communities they serve, and then you can hold them accountable. There is no easy way to "fix" things, but opening up communication and listening for the voices that will be affected will point law enforcement in the right direction.

Summary

The Dear Officer section utilized letters sent to the author and was answered using understanding of the law, and experience. The letters incorporated were used due to the nature of their questions, which were general enough to answer regardless of the geographical location. Please get familiar with your state laws as it applies to scenarios that may be similar in nature. The circumstances in each case vary, and it is important to understand that one "little" detail can cause a situation to have a different ending. The nature of the events were addressed examining any potential criminal aspects; however, not every situation in which an officer is present will result in criminal charges. The totality of a circumstance may or may not result in criminal charges. It was not the intent of the author to suggest that every encounter with officer's equal arrest or charges.

The black community faces a crucial time in society right now, and it is imperative that this community start to empower themselves for change. It is tough to look in the self-reflective mirror and hold oneself accountable. Although it is difficult to be brutally honest, it is needed for growth and direction. The black race has a history of pain and disappointment in this country, and this cannot be erased or the pain made light. It is crucial to heal from within, then to bind together as one, such as what has been done in black American history, which once created a reform. A race of people cannot ask for inclusion and fairness, yet segregate and discriminate among each other. This type of dysfunction is only detrimental to the immediate and future objectives of the race. Now this is not to say black people in America are not subject to criminal victimization, or racism on a higher level than any other ethnic group, for that would be lying. I also recognize that most black people are concerned with what goes on in their neighborhoods. There are countless, less visible marches and protest against black violence around this country. However empowerment is very much needed today more than ever. There are so many levels to uncover, if we are to improve the quality of life for our offspring's. I believe it begins with looking in the mirror and asking oneself if they hate being a part of the black race. Self-hate is a deceitful emotion for it clothes itself in false knowledge, wears masks of high self-esteem, walks in boots of self-righteousness, and crowns itself with inflated egos. Unification is begging to be let in, so let us open the door for understanding it will be accompanied by friends named honesty, self-reflection, realness, purity, and love.

Understanding your personal rights should not be an option but a must. It is important to understand how our Constitution protects us. Ignorance is a lack of knowledge, so let us seek more knowledge about our freedoms and our protections. Let us remember that everyone deserves to be protected, even the police that are employed to maintain law and order. There will be things in which police and civilians will not agree upon, which is why there is a judicial system that will have to answer the complicated questions and make clear things that are confusing. Even then, not everyone will agree with decisions made judicially. It is truly impossible to please everyone in any situation. This does not mean; we should not study and show ourselves approved by learning our rights federally, and locally. One can never fight an injustice if they don't know injustice occurred. What is worst is screaming something is unjust when indeed no injustice occurred. Then there are times when things just don't seem fair, I say patience is a virtue. History tells us that with time, wrongs are indeed made right eventually.

The police are a family; communities are a part of a family, there is blood bound families and there are emotionally connected families. In the times we are facing now, it is important to remember another family and that is the American family. We come from many different beliefs, ethnic backgrounds, religions, and walks of life; however, in the end, we are all a part of the same family, the human race family. This family should not be separated by race, class, ethnicity, or political party. Instead let us remember the things that bind us such as citizenship, whether natural or by naturalization. The ability to reach for the American dream, the fact that we are all humans, with red blood running through our veins. We are a family who enjoys the freedoms our Constitution affords us; we seek happiness, and we look to enhance our lives and the lives of loved ones. Our society has spent way too much time examining the differences. The definition of insanity according to Albert Einstein is "doing the same thing over and over again and expecting different results." Since examining differences have done nothing for our country but divided us, started wars and created societal chaos, let us do something different. Let's teach, preach, and remember what binds us, let's put our likeness in front of our differences for once.

It is always important to know where an organization came from and take note of the progression and development of such organization. History is examined in order to learn from mistakes, improve processes and move into an effective and efficient place of operation. Police in America has come a long way from volunteer workers who often slept on the job and chased missing animals, to paid workers who not only protect and serve their communities but partake in social community gathering to promote unity and peace. There is always an opportunity to improve and grow further and this is a time in policing where we are forced to look at processes, look at mistakes, open up communication and bring about understanding. It is now where we are forced to care, to listen, to pay attention, to cry, to feel growing pains and find ways to heal. We do this not because it is a choice but because societal times call for it. As our country has taught us, when it is time for change, change does not care who is for or against it, it will happen regardless.

Officers took the time to speak to civilians from an honest place. By not identifying their real names, they could speak freely about topics that included; profiling, training, media, quotas, myths about officers, and also share advice. This section allowed people to understand, the way in which officers thinks. Officers became transparent in order to expose the humanistic side of them. The insight given is valuable to understanding and remembering that officers want to do their jobs safely so that they, and you can go through your life without harm. No matter why an officer chooses this profession; most want to do their job and uphold the oath they swore to. Like any other profession, there will be a few terrible employees; however, unlike the "one bad apple spoils the bunch" philosophy, a few bad officers do not spoil the overall great work of officers across this country.

When it comes to police and community, there is no easy "fix" to the issues and misunderstanding that is present. The great thing about conflict is, it not end all be all, there is always hope of resolution. The end to a conflict comes when one side surrenders or when the last person is standing. Our society and our country cannot face a conflict of great proportions among civilians and the police that is called to protect, serve and to maintain the peace. Resolution will take the cooperation of both the police and the communities across this country. Resolution will come when both sides agree to forgive, to heal and to put love first. It may sound cliché, however, love really does cover all. Love has a way of lessening pain; it stuffs the holes made in the heart. It makes anger look foolish, and it brings about a peace that surpasses all understanding. Peace is desperately needed without apology right now. Let us wave the rainbow flag, which stands for peace and moves us to a better place collectively.

Terminology

Acquittal: A judgment that a person is not guilty of a crime in which that person has been charged.

Affidavit: A written statement confirmed by oath or affirmation, for use as evidence in court.

Arraignment: The action of arraigning someone in court: introduction of a case in court.

Arrest Citation: When you are handed a citation and free to go, in lieu of physical arrest. One is also filled out when there is a physical arrest as well.

BOLO: acronym for Be on the Look Out

Excessive Force: An officer's use of force is extreme when it is likely to result in *unjustifiable* great bodily harm or serious injury (based on totality of circumstance).

Guilty: Responsible for a specified wrongdoing.

Indictment: A formal charge or accusation of a serious crime.

Intent: When someone is determined to do something, intentionally or purposefully.

Not Guilty: Innocent, especially of a formal charge.

Obstruction (of justice): Attempt to hinder the discovery, apprehension, conviction or punishment of anyone who has committed a crime (can include bribery, murder, intimidation and use of physical force against witnesses, law enforcement officers or court officials.)

Perp: short for Perpetrator of a crime

Probable Cause: Reasonable grounds for making a search, pressing a charge.

Profiling: The analysis of a person's behavioral and psychological characteristics to predict or assess their capabilities in a certain situation; to identify a particular subgroup of people.

Reasonable Articulate Suspicion (RAS): (lesser than probable cause) sufficient to justify brief stops and detentions, but not enough to justify a full search.

What If

(This section addresses some common questions asked in greater detail and applies to everyone regardless of state)

What if...... I missed a court date for a ticket I received, and I am afraid I might have a warrant.

First thing is, if it is determined that there is a warrant for your arrest; the Judge is the only person that can clear that warrant. Your best bet is to get your affairs in order, if you have children make sure someone can watch them while you handle your business. Do not delay the inevitable, put the power in your own hands by controlling the outcome as much as you possible can by setting your affairs in order, then go to court and explain your situation. It is always better to go in instead of being taken in, when it wouldn't matter, the inconvenience caused.

What if....... The police knock at my door and ask if they can search my house.

Officers with a warrant will not ask you if they can search your house. They will show you their warrant (you should get a copy of it) and proceed with their search. If the officers do not have a warrant, you have the right to say no. There are some exceptions to the "don't have a warrant," say the person who is in control of the property consents to a search without being tricked or coerced, a search of your home will be legal. If an officer has the right to be at your home, example, they were in your house on a domestic call and observes illegal drugs in plain sight; they can take what they observed for evidence without a warrant. If the officer believes that there are more drugs in the home, they will have to get a warrant to search the rest of the property, but they will have probable cause to get that warrant. If exigent circumstances exist, this is considered an emergency situation where the process of getting a valid search warrant would compromise public safety or lead to the loss of evidence,' officers will have a right to search your home without a warrant. A search which is incident to arrest, also allows officers to search without a warrant. An example is if you are arrested in your house and the officers check other accomplices for weapons, which is known as a protective sweep, this is legal. This does not allow officers to start searching the entire house. There are different ways to which this situation could change; however, provided are the basics of how search warrants work.

What if……. I am presented with a search warrant at my home.

When an officer presents a search warrant, they are looking for specific items or people. These items will be listed in the warrant. So, for instance, say the warrant has items listed such as a large television, mid-sized painting, a game console and a home stereo system. The searching officers can look into any area where these items can be concealed. Some dresser draws or small spaces would not be feasible places for officers to check since the listed items would not be able to fit in those spaces. Say the warrant has a ring listed, then the officers can look ANYWHERE a ring could be concealed. You can image that would be in most places within your home. If the warrant is for a person, officers can look anywhere a person can hide.

What if……. I am pulled over by an unmarked vehicle with lights and sirens.

Most states have policies in place that doesn't allow unmarked police vehicles to make stops. However, there are some states in which unmarked vehicles are utilized for traffic. If you are being pulled over by a vehicle that is not clearly marked, don't just ignore the car. When you pull over you can ask the uniformed or non-uniformed person for two pieces of police identification (do not be indignant with the person). You can also phone 911 and inform them that you are being pulled over by a vehicle that you are not sure is a police vehicle, and want to have them on the line for your safety. Pull over in a well-lit area if possible. Increasing your speed and trying to "get away" will only put yourself and the general public in dire straits.

About the Author

Dani was born the second child to the Late Carole Ann Nelson and the Late Raymond Lee Harris in the Bronx, New York on March 28. Dani was reared in Harlem New York with four siblings. Raised by a single mother, in the impoverished Johnson Projects in Harlem NY was the start of life for Dani. The projects where a sobering reminder of what Dani so desperately wanted to escape on a daily basis. Dani excelled in school making it an escape from the harsh normal surroundings of everyday living. Growing up on welfare and at times eating oatmeal cookies for dinner, Dani felt early on that life could be cruel. Alcoholism, physical abuse and anger seemed to be the things Dani faced on a daily basis. Having watched their father slice their mother's neck from ear to ear, Dani never developed the safe haven mentality, for there was always some adversity to deal with. Shuffling through the foster care system, jumping from one older half sibling to another then finally to a step mother who attempted to create a safe haven environment, it was at the age of 15 that Dani was reunited with family under the same roof. Fighting anger, resentment and depression, Dani moved out of the home at the age of 16 and one year later Dani's mother passed away from Lupus after being diagnosed with AIDS. Dani and the older sister decided to raise the younger siblings and shed them from further foster care living.

At the age of 24, Dani almost became a statistic after being shot in the face at point blank range. Already dealing with anger issues, the shooting further pushed Dani to a low point in life. Bouncing back from the despairs of life, Dani made a turnaround, joining the Law Enforcement community and decided to be a productive citizen. Turning the trials of life into testimonies about hope, determination, self-belief, and never giving up Dani found a gift in motivating others to look at life from a different perspective than the one that is handed to us. Life is truly what you make it, is the model that gives Dani the courage to face tribulations and strife and turn them into victorious moments in life.

Dani obtained an associate's degree in 2002, after taking a five year break in education, returned to school to obtain Bachelors of Science, Masters of Human Resource Management and Doctorate of Business Administration degrees. Dani has found passion in motivating and encouraging others. Dani has been invited to speak at local law enforcement agencies, Universities and Churches. Facing adversity as a minority, Dani lives to show others how to find inner peace in the midst of personal storms. How to find your personal passion and serve others in order to live a complete and fulfilled life. Topics in which Dani frequently speak on include but is not limited to the following.

- Interpersonal Communication

- Law Enforcement and minorities

- Gay Panic Defence

- Intersex: What Is It?

- Multiculturalism

- Domestic Violence

- Accepting one another's differences

- People Management

- Crystal Meth and its impact

- Sound ethics in today's time

145

- Gun violence

- PTSD (post-traumatic stress syndrome)

- HIV/AIDS

Made in the USA
Charleston, SC
04 March 2015